Tred Parris, known to his friends as Freddie, has been married for 54 years with two children and five grandchildren. He has been retired for about eleven years. He is a beekeeper and enjoys his allotments with his wife, Georgina, as well as dancing, walking, art and playing his ukulele. He has written several articles for local publications.

KIND REGARDS
ALAN AN Pat

Tred PARRIS

22/4/22

Tred Parris

FOUGHT A MILLION BATTLES

Normally Home for Tea

AUSTIN MACAULEY PUBLISHERS™

LONDON • CAMBRIDGE • NEW YORK • SHARJAH

A CIP catalogue record for this title is available from the British Library.

ISBN 9781398410626 (Paperback)
ISBN 9781398410633 (ePub e-book)

www.austinmacauley.com

First Published 2022
Austin Macauley Publishers Ltd®
1 Canada Square
Canary Wharf
London
E14 5AA

I would like to thank my wife, Georgina, who sat by me night after night, guiding my appalling attempts at mastering the keyboard, making suggestions on how some aspects of the book might be couched and her incredible memory of notable events.

Prologue

These following pages are some of my recollections from my time serving as a territorial army volunteer (TAVR), with whom I served in one form or another from 1968 to early 1984. They are from my fading memory without the aid of a diary but with some research and the odd photographs. Nevertheless, if some people and places and dates have got mixed up or caused any offence, I apologise.

None of this would have happened without the huge contribution of support, sacrifice and love from my wife, Georgina, who at times I did not deserve but will be eternally grateful to.

My period of service came between the country's major war fighting conflicts. My only opportunity to become directly involved came towards the end of my service in 1982 when the Falklands War broke out. I, like many others, volunteered as soon as the news first broke, only to be refused immediately. This was not entirely unexpected as the reserve forces covenant's mobilisation, at the time, could only be decreed by the government in a national emergency. Nevertheless, it still stung a bit and underlines the feeling that many reservists feel that they are looked down on by their regular counterparts as somehow not worthy, to wear the same badge and beret. I experienced this myself and at one point was virtually ostracised by the members of my sister's regular regiment when attached to them. (*Squaddies gripe over and I digress!*)

There was, however, a great deal of other 'stuff' that had been going on, to a lesser degree in Africa, South America, Germany and the troubles. So although my final 'hurrah' did not materialise, I like to think that we volunteers contributed in many ways to the greater good, even if only a few of us ever fired our weapons in anger at my time.

A lot of these *contributions* are not covered in these pages, nor are the volunteers' full names mentioned in the following pages. Not through enforcement, as I have my 'letter of disclosure' but because the mantra of 'need to know' is still in my breast, also after the first Iraq war and the publications that followed caused a great deal of furore in the SAS; many of us have signed an affidavit to say what others who did not need to know then, do not need to know now.

I realise that your view of the volunteers who go to work every day when they are not in uniform, managing the triangle of family, army and work, may be skewed as a result. But in the end, appreciate our contribution and at times bring a smile to your lips, for without humour many hardships could not be endured.

Tred Parris

December 2019

Fought a Million Battles, Normally Home for Tea!

I always liked to think of myself as a patriot and was willing to do my bit, but looking back at my reason for joining the Territorials it was for money! The patriotism and commitments all came later.

At the time I was working as a T2B (*lowest of the low!*) for the GPO – part of a team of four – we had one of those green lorries you used to see trundling about with a couple of telegraph poles stuck on top. Well, we used to put them up or do repairs to underground cables and the like. One of my colleagues – I shall call him 'Dave' – told me he was a TAVR for the Royal Corps of Transport as it was then. He attended 'drill'* once a week, did one day's training a month and a two-week 'camp' once a year. My ears pricked up when he said he got paid, and a yearly bonus of £100.00!

At the time, we had not long been married, we both worked. Georgina was very often out working at night hosting the 'Pippa Dee' parties that were popular at the time to help contribute to the household budget. I can't remember how much I earned but the clincher for me was that I used our ancient multi-coloured Thames van to drive the seven miles from home to Bletchley Park where the GPO was based and on my way back,[1] often ran out of petrol, mid or towards the end of the week, depending if we used it over the weekend. When it did, I left it abandoned wherever it was until the next pay day when armed with a can full of petrol, I walked back to it, and the whole process started again, so a bit of extra cash sounded very inviting!

I had always been interested in all things military so with Georgina's blessing, I started looking around and found a Royal Artillery Medium Battery in Leagrave, near Luton, within easy striking distance at the time. Calling ahead, I went over on their 'drill night' and saw their PSI*. During our chat, the subject of parachuting came up, something medium batteries of guns did not do! The PSI must have seen the interest in my eyes. He started telling me with a smirk that the nearest unit that did parachuting was at Hitchin and they got paid an extra 50p a day! In due course, I found myself in the squadron office of C Squadron 21 SAS(V), a place I was to become very familiar in the years ahead.

Their PSI said, with a welcoming smile, I would be welcome* (*what did he know*!) but I would have to do something called 'Selection and Continuation'. I had never heard of the 'Special Air Service', so I said, "Okay, where do I sign?"

---

[1] Incredibly you could join straight from civvy street at the time

Selection

So a few weeks later, a buff Ministry of Defence rail warrant dropped through our letterbox with an accompanying letter inviting me to attend the Duke of York's HQ, London, for a medical, to be sworn in and sign the official secrets act!

Going to London was something of an experience for a small-town boy like me. Going for a 'big night out' to the Wilton Hall in nearby Bletchley was considered a special event, never mind medicals and secrets acts! Nevertheless, I found myself with several other hopefuls, some of whom came from 'C' Squadron so I was not alone. The first glimmer of bonding came that day when one of the hopefuls asked the person in front of him whose eyes were being tested to remember the top line as his were a bit dodgy! We all passed and spent the rest of the day being kitted out with OG trousers[2], woolly pulleys[3], a para smock, boots, gaiters, a cap comforter, 44-pattern webbing, which looked impossible to fathom out, poncho and sleeping bag, as well as a kit bag, bergen rucksack[4], shirts hairy and a draws cellular! The following Wednesday, me and the other, I think eight, recruits, paraded for the first time at Hitchin. Falling in behind the squadron lads, I made myself presentable as I could with my new clothes, but looking around, the others looked like something the cat dragged in! Looking in awe at some of the sqn lads who, with the exception of the few who

---

[2] OGs, Trousers known as 'Olive Greens.'

[3] Woolly pully is a heavy-duty jumper

[4] The bergen rucksack, originally designed for skiing, had a triangular frame that the back and shoulder straps were attached to.

never would, were all smartly dressed, 'falling in' with practiced ease to the stand-at-ease for the evening muster parade.

Over the next few Wednesday drill nights, we were shown how to dress, do simple drill manoeuvres, such as falling in, in some sort of order, standing at ease and coming to attention when your name was called out replying, "Here sir." We got our eager hands, for the first time, on the army's standard SLR[5]. We started being taught map reading and went out on map to obtain ground familiarisation, on the nearby Hexton Hills, where we could see a huge area of land to the north. We could then look at our maps and use our compass to find some points on the map such as a church or wood. From these basics, we went on to learning to do 'back bearings[6]', a triangular method of establishing your exact location in the days before the advent of the satellite navigator. Fitness training was also part of our regular routine. Our instructor was the formidable Sgt Dereck. He was one of the few soldiers who had served in all three SAS regiments, (22, 23 and 21), so he was a very experienced man; he was also a demon Joker! One drill night, we were instructed to pick up one of long former benches we had in the drill hall between us and follow Dereck out of the hall, at the double! Turning left, we jogged the quarter or so mile to the nearby park, did a circuit and followed by squats jumps, push ups, etc. before setting off back.

---

[5] SLR – self-loading rifle weighed about 10lbs with a 20-round magazine.

[6] Back bearings – a method of pinpointing your position.

As we neared the gates, we swung out expecting to go in when Dereck went straight past! The groans and gasps were audible! Just about clinging on by this time, we did another mile or so before returning, hoping that we would go this time. Thankfully, we did collapse on and around the benches that became synonymous with sweat and hard breathing over the coming weeks and months.

A few weeks later, our first weekend loomed; this was the start of the 'Selection and Continuation' and the first weekend of many I would leave Georgina on her own for what I had so glibly signed up to! We were briefed on arrival along with the other recruits that there would be three weekends, fortnightly. Followed by three in the Brecon Beacons, and then two weeks at the Parachute Battle School situated in Brecon itself. The first three were all where we were all assembled on the South Downs meeting up with the other budding band of brothers to form the selection course, 1/68.

This consisted of instructions on how to assemble the '44' webbing, pack our bergen, so that essentials you might need were readily accessible at the top and dry clothes, socks and the vital sleeping bag, all inside a plastic bag at the bottom. We had to cook the contents of the dried food in our twenty-four-hour ration packs. We then set off on what was to be another first for me, cross-country walking, carrying my steel framed bergen rucksack. This was led by one of our directing staff (DS), stopping to do map reading, taking back bearings, estimating distances, reading our maps and the like when we stopped for a 'brew'. The walk was about ten miles, coming to an end in the late afternoon, then putting up a 'Basha'[7] for the first time and learning from the uncomfortable night that followed how important a good spot, if you could find one, was! The second weekend was a full day march now as individuals, carrying a minimum of 35lbs in our bergen, a belt kit with water, a compass pouch, twenty-four hours of emergency food and a tiny first aid kit. There was another night leg tagged on starting after the last light. The South Downs were a fairly safe training area, as all the walking was along the back of the Downs. Looking down from the ridge, the lights of the coastal towns could be seen clearly to the south and with pylons marching across the countryside in the right direction; it was hard to get lost. But some did and on the third weekend, some faces were already missing!

---

[7] Basha means shelter in Malay language.

Weekend three, by now it was early March, Georgina was heavily pregnant, the baby was overdue and she had gone into Aylesbury Hospital. The weekend was more of the same, only further both in the day and at night; I was, by this time, a confident navigator and was taking to this like a duck to water! My only drama was that to my horror I went to draw my map from within my para smock to find it was not there! Thinking where it might have fallen out, I had no choice but to go back to a hedge I had clambered through, and to my relief, I found it. Assembly on the Sunday morning lay by on the busy London to Brighton; road several bodies were already on the three-tonner parked waiting for us. Not all had made it or had 'Jacked'!

I was obviously desperate to get home and decided to head straight for the hospital, arriving mid-afternoon to find my lovely wife distraught because the baby had been still born! To make matters worse, she was not even in a side ward but just had a screen around her so could hear all the happy mums, babies and visitors' laughter! Even after all these years, writing these lines tears are running down my cheeks; heaven knows what impact the loss made to Georgina. A lesser person, I am sure, would have crumbled into despair. Although later, she would very often weep when I left her, she never once asked me to give up on what was now my quest.

The Brecons

Then came our first visit to the Wales, the historic stamping ground for the regiment since its resurrection in the 1950*. By now, the weight we were expected to carry was 40lbs plus our belt kit. We started in the Black Mountains and walking was much the same as before, as far as navigation was concerned as was South Downs. The distance had increased and there was considerably more climbing up onto the ridge.

From then onto the Brecon Beacons, the practice of not knowing when you had arrived at the last rendezvous (RV)* started to be used. Arriving at an RV, very often you may be asked a question like, "Point out a church with a steeple on the map," or, "What is the height you are at now?" You were expected to be properly dressed, stating your name and address the instructor as 'Staff'. On occasion, your bergen would be weighted and the penalty of being underweight was a large autographed stone to carry to your next RV, given a six-figure grid reference, a quick check confirming you knew where it was on your map and off you went on the next leg.

The Beacons, for those not familiar with, is in the Welsh National Park; it is dominated by 'Pen Y Fan' and its 2,907 ft top, which can be seen from most of the park, and on a clear day, as far back as the Black Mountains we had so recently walked. Surrounded by other only slightly less formidable peaks, each inter sped with deep valleys, rivers and reservoirs. Our regiment made full use of these ups and downs to plan the various routes the recruits would be expected to complete.

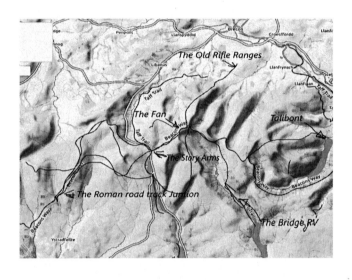

*The Brecons and selection routes for 1/68
All the SAS Regiments were disbanded at the end of WWII.

Arriving at the Story Arms car park very late Friday night, we made our 'bashas' as best we could, with orders to parade at 0700 the next morning, ready to move. Looking up, I could see the dark silhouettes of the mountains surrounding us; this filled me with foreboding at what lay ahead, a sensation that never left me, even after I had joined. After a restless uncomfortable night in sloping tree roots of the woods adjacent to Story Arms car park, I paraded with the others, standing behind our bergens in the 'at ease' position for our briefing in the cold grey Welsh morning, cap comforters pulled down and the collars of our parachute regiment smocks turned up. We were briefed, then split into groups under an instructor to start another conducted walk. With Sgt Derek once again our leader, we set off, leaving the car park, first coming across a stream that ran down from the distant peaks. Our leader told us that this was where were going to get some 'Welsh wax' on our boots and promptly walked across the stream looking back to make sure we followed; later, we discovered nearby rocks that could be used as stepping stones, and much later still a bridge was built. So with soggy boots, we started up on the first of many accents of the 'fan' the track at that time could only be walked in a single file. Later, walking on my own at night, it was quite difficult to follow; you could easily wander off on the broad, fairly feature-less, sides up to the mountain, something I did on several occasions.

But on our first visit in daylight with a leader, there were no such problems, apart from trying to draw enough breath to keep your position in the column; my tactic at that time was simply looking down at the man's legs and feet in front of me, making sure the distance remained the same. The accent took us about an hour, thankfully arriving on the saddle and the last of the serious climbing before walking up on up to the trig point itself on the flat top. From here, there was, on a clear day, a superb vista right across the Beacons, something I never tired of.

A much later squadron picture in the 1980s

Then, we went down the extremely steep and precarious south side to the old disused rail track, following it thankfully along its gently sloping grass to the bridge RV at the top of what is now called the 'Taff Trail'. After a break, we set off back up the track to the 'fan', climbing the last of which required all four limbs, before descending once again back down to the Story Arms late in the afternoon. Exhausted, but with a couple of hours before we had orders to parade again, cooking up a curry, one of many more to come! I rolled out my sleeping bag, and using my belt kit as a pillow, slept the sleep of the dead!

As the light began to fail, we assembled around the back of the three-tonner and were given our final RV for the night march and being checked each knew where it was. With the causeway over the Talybont Reservoir to the East, we set off into the gathering gloom. Stopping to study my map under the light of red filtered light from my G10[8] torch, I could see it involved the first half of the day's walk, but then climbing again to and follow the escarpment to a trig point over the Talybont causeway, followed by a steep descent down where the RV would be. Or, I surmised following all of the first half down to near the Taff Trail, where I saw on the map, there was a disused tunnel marked that ran *under* the bottom of the mountain, coming out at the southern of Talybont; it was longer but no climbing!

I made my decision, as it turned out, so did some others. Arriving at the tunnel entrance, I was mortified to find it was blocked! But on closer inspection, I found a single door, stepping inside to total eerie blackness with just the sound of dripping water to keep me company. Taking the filter off my torch, I started picking my way over the assorted detritus on what then seemed an endless odyssey; I kept following the beam of my torch in the pitch-blackness until I suddenly coming across the other end of the tunnel. It was again blocked, but, to my relief, also with a small access door. This let me out into a cold clear night to finish my night march arriving in the early hours of Sunday morning. Already onboard the three-tonner were the others who had made it back, then transported back to the Story Arms totally exhausted.

Sunday morning held nothing more demanding than a debriefing; not all had made it back or were 'Jacked'. Then the three-hour drive in the back of the freezing, windy

---

[8] G10 Torch standard Army issue.

smoke-filled lorry, in which we were rocking in and out of sleep, many in their sleeping bags on the coconut-matting floor, others huddled, with hoods up swaying to and fro as we hurtled back up the A40 and the TA centre. Arriving and lowering myself down, my legs felt so stiff and cold that fearing they might snap if I jumped! Then climbing gingerly into our car to drive the fifty minutes' drive home to Georgina, a shower, food and lovemaking before falling asleep next to her lovely, warm, soft body exhausted.

Monday morning back to work!

Two weeks later, we were back. The routine was now established: kissing Georgina goodbye, loading my bergen in the car for the drive to Hitchin, meeting the others and the ride in the three-tonner back to the Story Arms. Sometimes we stopped for fish and chips in Burford or nearby surprising the locals, barging in bleary eyed for cod and chips and then arriving again very late on Friday night looking like the others for a flat spot in the woods to sleep as best under my basha. Then the Saturday morning 0700 parade for the briefing and bergen weigh-in. This time, it was 'three times over', virtually no navigation required, provided the weather stayed fine. Up to the RV on the 'fan', report in, then down to the RV at the top of the Taff Trail, back up to the top, down again, following the many false peaks on the north side to the old disused ranges at the bottom. Arriving there, my legs were wobbly from the long downhill descent, finding our sergeant lolling up the wheel of a Land Rover in the early afternoon sunshine. Reporting in, he simply smirked, raised his hand and pointed back up! A last exhausting climb back to the top and a final jog down to the Story Arms to what would be the final RV. The reporting in was after nine and a half hours.

Our last weekend in the Brecons was the dreaded 'Long Drag', all we knew was that it was indeed going to be very long, walking from one RV to another until you were told you had finished! I never knew quite how long the 'drag' was but I completed it in nineteen and a half hours, which was, as it turned out, half an hour inside the cut off time. The record was set that day of twelve and a half hours by one of my fellow recruits from 'D' squadron in Portsmouth. The exact distance remained a mystery to me, but if my cross-country speed was about two miles per hour (*one mile an hour up, three* j*ogging down*) that would make it, give or take, just short of 40 miles.

Next stop was the selection 'camp', packing for the expected two weeks and saying goodbye to Georgina, I set off once again to Hitchin and whatever lay ahead. We were based at the Parachute Battle School Brecon. As it turned out, the 'test' week was pretty well all the same as we had done before, although a speed march was added at some point, being double marched as a group for five miles or so.

This was to be followed by the planned continuation training for those that passed. The first walk was starting at the causeway on our old friend, the Talybont Reservoir, an almost reverse of what we had done before, but this time in daylight and timed. The process was climbing up to the trig point, then walking to the first RV at the bridge on the Taff Trail, up over the fan down and to the Story Arms. Looking back, using the old railway tunnel when walking the route the other way around, was the cause of my impending demise because somehow, I got myself well off route.

23

Finally arriving at the RV much later in the afternoon was good for me, finding two of the four remaining from the 'C' squadron sitting behind the DS* staff, on their bergens, obviously out of the running. Falling for one of the oldest ruses I used myself many years later to tell a recruit that he was so far behind, there was no way he was going to get to the next RV in time. "You might as well 'Jack now'!" the DS staff told me. Looking up the valley to the fan, it looked a very long way away in the late afternoon shadow. Agreeing without giving it much thought, unslinging my beregn, sat down; I was out. finished. I had just jacked, Instantly regretting my decision, but it was too late!

I then spent the next couple of embarrassing days with the other failures doing dishes in the cookhouse until there was sufficient number for transport to be laid on back to our various squadrons. Handing my kit in and returning home, feeling slightly shell shocked and very dejected at the turn of events.

Green Jacket!

Not long after my failed selection attempt, casting about found a platoon of the Royal Green Jackets 4th Volunteer Battalion based in nearby Bletchley.

Joining the Green Jackets, I knew as little about them as I had about the SAS(V). I Discovered that they were a light infantry outfit[9] with a history dating back to the American wars of independence. At the time, the TAVR was going through a major review, so although my first contact was at Bletchley, never attending there, but reported to Aylesbury where the newly formed three Platoon of 4 Royal Green Jackets (4 RGJ) were based in Oxford Road Aylesbury. The

---

[9] They were formed from the old County regiment, the Ox & Bucks light infantry. They had been the first to wear green and to use the skirmish line*, doing away at a stroke with the British Army's suicidal wearing of RedCoats and marching in serried ranks at the enemy guns! They also were the first to use the mini ball*, as opposed to the 'Brown Bess*'. These changes made the RGJ, who marched at 140 paces* to the minute, a valuable, flexible and fast-moving unit. They along with other later light infantry units were all part of what was called the 'Light Division' at the time, now all amalgamated into the 'Rifles'.

platoon was one of three all part of 'A' company which had its headquarters in Oxford. In due course, I drew my clothes, webbing, helmet and other paraphernalia, including an old-style greatcoat and ancient respirator, but no 'draws cellula', all stuffed in a kitbag.

Although a new boy found myself slotting into the platoon, I had a long way to go before I would be a competent infantry soldier, but a lot of the basics I had from my experience on selection all stood me in step. Not long after joining, learned that the battalion was gearing up for its annual camp at Folkstone. For me and other new boys, it would be a 'recruits camp' and once again, I would be leaving Georgina and, by then, my young son to their own devices for a couple of weeks, so I said goodbye once again to my long-suffering partner and baby son, Kelly.

She must have been thinking, *Here we go again!* Len, an established TA soldier and lance corporal came to pick me up. He became a sort of mentor in those two weeks and has since gone on to become one of my life-long friends. If he ever reads these lines, I owe him a debt of gratitude and several beers. I make a special mention of Len because as we progressed through the ranks, he was always one rank in front of me, until both of us received our royal warrants when promoted to warrant officer class-two; even then he was promoted before me, and still likes to remind me all these years later that he has seniority!

New boy and small son!   *Persian Gulf*

All this was to stand me in good stead in the future. I loved it, slotting right into the platoon, and I soon became an established member, enjoying the physical side of the march and shoots, assault courses, weapons training as well as the camaraderie and social side of men, who soon became my friends. Learning a great deal about both myself during those two weeks as well as a lot about the basics of dress, equipment, weapons and tactics, all part of the infantry lifeblood.

After we came back from Folkestone with the welcome reuniting with my family, the weekend training went on. One of those lessons I was never to forget was when training to fight in a built-up area in the deserted 'Imber Village*'. I meant to throw a thunder flash *(a simulated grenade)* into a windowless house only for it to bounce back from the frame and land at my feet where it went off with a very large bang!

You only do that sort of thing once!

27

In June 1969, the battalion was deployed to the Isle of Man. We boarded a train and a ferry to move up to Liverpool. The battalion formed up on the busy station looking almost like one of those wartime pictures of a troop train, and it drew many a stare. Once we arrived at the Altcar Training Camp on the Isle of Man, our home for the duration, training went on much the same but with the battalion together on a much larger scale.

The island's TT races were on at the time, so road movement was restricted to certain times of the day. Frequently, we could hear the screaming of high revving engines as the bikes tore around the twisty twenty-two-mile road circuit.

I was told by my platoon sergeant several days into our camp to report to the company commander, who to my alarm, tasked me to meet an incoming army air force helicopter and 'Recce'* forward to find a lager (*a suitable stop for the night)* for the company that night. The chopper duly arrived in dramatic style, pivoting around close to the ground in preparation to depart. It was one of those now ancient types, a Bell 47, with a large bubble canopy for the pilot and in this case, a very nervous situation for me. The company commander must have thought mistakenly off me as (*probably due to my recent history)* a competent navigator,

I had no experience of helicopters, but at the same time, I did not want to lose face by showing my inexperience, clambering into the cockpit and donned the headphones to cut out the hammering of the engine just behind us, gave my thumbs up to 'Biggles', the engine note changed and we lifted off on our quest. The topography of the hills and dales of the island were quite easy to read from the ground level, but as we gained altitude, these all flattened into one. To make matters worse, we had gone around in a large circle and I had not got a clue where we were or in what direction we were facing (*something that is common to helicopter operations*). Pressing my throat mic, I said as much to the pilot but neither had he! Soon a road came into view as we flew across the countryside. At my suggestion, we decided to follow it, within minutes coming to crossroads with a signpost. We went down to the hover and, no doubt made several motorists' hearts beat faster, reading the names on the post. At that point, picking up where the nearby names on the map were spread on my knees, I was able to give my pilot the thumbs up and indicate with my hand the direction we needed to go. Shortly after that, finding a good spot for the company was then quite easy. Returning like some hero to the gaggle that had gathered to welcome the returning helicopter. Climbing out it immediately departed and ran back, donning my beret, and reported to the company commander. He seemed very impressed, having no idea of our adventures and mistakenly securing my shaky expertise as some sort of ace navigator. Later in the camp, there was the closing exercise. The full battalion was involved, giving officers and men alike the chance to train as one cohesive unit. I, now thought of as being an expert navigator, was tasked with leading a night-time 'fighting patrol'* to attack our 'enemy', a small group of regulars from the third battalion.

Shortly after we set off, we ran into hill fog and shortly after that, I was lost! We never found the enemy, and with my reputation in tatters, returned to our lines with tails between our legs and my 'mate' Len never let me forget it even to this day!

From time to time, the battalion held junior and NCO (*Non-commissioned Officer*) cadres. Mine was for a junior NCO position and held over a weekend at the company HQ in Oxford. All weekend training, of course, meant preparing homework in the week, coming home on a Friday, something to eat, kissing goodbye to the family and driving in this case to Oxford. I had two full days of training in commanding troops, lectures on procedure and so on, arriving back home late in the evening on Sunday. Shortly after, the cadre was promoted to lance corporal. Now proudly wearing my new single dark-green stripe, I became second in command of my rifle section and in charge of the 'gun group' (*the section's machine gun*).

In January 1970, the battalion was off again to Sharjah in the Trucial Oman States. It was my first experience of the desert. Descending to land, my first impressions out of the window of the prop-driven Britannia aircraft as it circled, with the undercarriage rumbling dawn and flaps extending, was of a spectacular endless sea of sand stretching out looking a reddish brown in the early morning sunlight, something I never got tired of seeing, although later well aware of how the cool morning light soon transferred into a hot blazing midday heat!

Based in the town, my recollections were of a dusty downtrodden place, with a lot of dirty white single-storey buildings; it had a single road that stretched out into the desert coming to a dead stop after some twenty miles, where it was surrounded by several cars that had either ran out of petrol or had been abandoned as unwanted. On the road out in the back of several beat-up old lorries, probably left over the war, we passed quite a few Arabs walking alongside the road, some with camels, other with heavily laden donkeys. We had been told that it was bad manners to wave with your left hand because that was the hand Arabs used to clean themselves after using the toilet (*I use the word loosely!*). Needless to say, each one that returned our salutations as we passed by, used their left hand.

We were based at a *wadi* out in the desert that had running water for pretty much all of the ten days. We trained in what the navy calls tropical routine, meaning leaving early in the morning to train in all the basics that were our bread and butter, ending at around midday until early

31

evening because of the heat. Then more of the same as the day cooled. The difference in temperature between the heat of the day and the cold of the night was remarkable. On guard duty, just before dawn, a cap comforter, gloves and the collar turned up on your great coat was a must!

One day, doing an advance to contact, our section came to a halt, taking cover behind whatever was available. A voice from my left said, "Corporal can I move?" I asked why he said that. The reply was, "Cos there's a f…ing great black snake sharing this rock with me!"

One day, the medical officer came round, giving us instructions on the need for salt to replace what we were losing through our excursions. He handed out two tablets each; me being me, chucked them both in my mouth and swallowed. A look of horror came over the doc's face. "You supposed to dissolve them in your water bottle," he shouted. I was then ordered, to the laughs and jeers from the assembled platoon, to drink the contents of my water bottle, then jump up and down to dissolve them in my stomach.

Towards the end of our time, there was the usual major exercise. I can't recall who were the 'enemy'. I never saw them anyway, but lying spread out along an escarpment, we had a visit from our commanding officer along with a couple of other officers. He came to stand alongside me, surveying the lower ground in front of our position. Turning on my side, I said, "Excuse me sir, but you are sky-lining our position." He mumbled his apology and retreated, but later I had a very large flea in my ear, for embarrassing the colonel, from our platoon sergeant, Tony!

3 Platoon on patrol gun group at the rear.

Returning one day from training, we found the local Arabs, taking advantage of our inexperience and deserted camp, had stolen five tents! We found it quite amusing at the time, but I bet the colonel is still filling-in forms today! In the last few days, we had some free time and I went into the bazar to buy a 'Persian' rug to take home. Later, learning that my wife thought it was horrid, after a short period, it disappeared never to be seen again!

While I was trying to negotiate with the stallholder, another Arab came to stand by me, dressed in a traditional dish dash, complete with headgear and a huge brown Arabic nose; he said in plain English, "Don't panic, mate, I will sort it out for you." Well, you could have knocked me down with a feather!

But sort it out he did! Parading on the last day, two 'Pinkies'[10], long wheel-based Land Rovers, equipped with long-range fuel tanks, sand boards and radios, each manned with four sunburnt soldiers, drove by. Bristling with weapons and radio aerials waving to and fro, they sped off out towards the Saudi border.

I immediately identified them as SAS and it brought back all the rancour of my failure and I resolved then to try selection again as two attempts at selection were allowed.

So despite a very nice letter from the colonel asking me to reconsider, I requested a leave of absence and transfer to the 21 SAS(V) to attempt selection again. But this time as a much more capable person!

---

[10] The Pinkies were so named because of their desert camouflage of pink.

Second Time Around

My second attempt very nearly did not happen. Parading for the first time, I still wore my infantry style combat suit complete with the stripe and green beret, not knowing that no rank or insignia is allowed; all are supposed to be equal for the forthcoming coming tests. Two full screws[11] (army slang for corporals) part of the directing staff, I could see out of the corner of my eye, were making a beeline for me! They ordered me to remove my beret and don a cap comforter, then drawing a knife, one made to start cutting the stripe off my arm. Thinking this was well out of order, I refused, but was offered to fall out and remove the offending item before re-joining the muster parade. This was allowed by the WOII in charge, but of course, I had made two enemies who were going to make me pay dearly for the incident.

By then, being quite experienced and considerably fitter, I found the South Downs weekends not much more than a refresher. Navigation was made even easier as the routes were much as before, still physically demanding in places, but well within my abilities. It was more by luck than judgement, the staying out of trouble, until we came to the

---

[11] 'Full screws' is British Army slang for corporals.

second weekend in the Brecons and the first time we were walking as individuals (again for me). Approaching the back of the three-tonner being used as an RV, I saw, with some trepidation, the two corporals, with whom earlier I had fallen foul of at the first muster parade, were manning it. They decided I was not dressed correctly and ordered me to do twenty press-ups. Annoyed but undeterred, I obeyed the order, carrying on to complete the weekend. But this behaviour did not stop; invariably, they would be at one or another RVs and each time found some reason for more punishment and delay for one day, they commanded me, in pouring rain, to do press ups in a large puddle of water. My patience snapped and I said, "No!" I was not going to do press ups in water, ensuring that the remainder of my day and night march would be done in soaking wet clothes was not acceptable!

They had already given me my next RV, so without having it checked to know where it was, I went on my way. Unknown to me, at the directing staff's debrief, at the end of the weekend, they wanted me sacked. The following Wednesday, I found myself called into the squadron office. The PSI by then, Norman Duggen, a long time regular coming to the end of his time, asked me what had gone on. I explained, admitting that refusing an order was not the right way to go about getting through selection, but I also explained why my refusal was, in my opinion, justified. The outcome was an admonishment but permission to carry on, and the two individuals never bothered me again.

Long drag came and went as long and exhausting as it had been the first time. Recalling that although this was supposed to be completed as individuals, inevitably you jogged along with others from time to time.

On one occasion, stopping for a brew and food, another guy stopped; we ate and talked before setting off, keeping each other company for a while. I was feeling quite low at the time and the company somehow picked me up. Later, I was able to do the same for someone else, meeting him tired and dispirited, but just a few words and invitation to walk along with me, he picked up, got the second wind and the next day, was amongst the finishers.

The 'test week' was basically a rerun of the last Brecon weekends with a few minor add-ons. But there was a difference, minor injuries can become major ones. There was no time to recover your energy before the next day's demands. For some, this proved too much and they withdrew because of one or the other maladies, or some like me to try again. Completing course 2/1970, about ten percent had passed from those who had originally volunteered, keeping what was the average for some years.

Us, who were left, went straight onto continuation. The aim of this really was as much about suitability to 'fit in' as well as various exercises at night, days on the ranges, minor tactics, river crossing and, including survival navigation, animal traps and trapping and resistance to interrogation.[12]

---

[12] Later there was first stepping stones then bridge

Continuation

My fingers were numb and shaking a little as I tied the last loop of paracord around the top of my improvised Bergen rucksack raft. Just inches from my soggy right knee in the mud, the dark, smooth, fast-flowing waters of the River Wye looked threatening in the late October night.

On the other side way off in the distant blackness, a very small single convoy light looked out with its red impassive eye from our transport. It seems to be waiting patiently, beckoning those that crosses to its safe interior with the ride back to the battle school. Our instructions were to get to the transport; those that did not would have to walk! Some we never saw again! (*failures were usually separated from those going on*).

Feeling for the muddy bottom with my plimsoll-covered foot, the cold water soaked through my OG trousers, then plunging in and dragging the raft with me, I struck out for the other side. The current and cold took my breath away, the dark outline of the bank swept past me at an alarming rate.

For what seemed ages later, the mass of the far bank was in front of me. Scrabbling, clawing and climbing up on the open field, I was relieved to be on dry land again. Grunts and gasps on either side of me told me they had made it too. In the distance, the small red unblinking light still waited patiently. Slinging my Bergen, I set off at a trot in the strange glow of warmth, which prevailed in the first few minutes, after getting onto dry land (*rapidly changing to freezing cold*). All around me, other dark shapes jogged along grunting under their loads across the field.

Without warning, I fell over in an almighty undignified crash. Confused, I caught my breath, struggling like some stranded whale when the object I had fell over let out an enormous *"mooooo"* and stood up, blotting out the moonlight! In a flash, I was up and running hard. I had fallen over a cow! Needless to say I was first back!

In the following days, we did training on minor tactics, an innocent little title that meant repeatedly throwing myself with the others up and down the moon grass of the Sennybridge ranges, with either a rifle or lugging the twenty-eight-pound general-purpose machine gun, my lungs bursting to fire at distant targets. This was all under the constant merciless snarling para-regiment instructors. Some of us had done this before in the units we came from of course, but the brutality of dead sheep caught in the crossfire was ignored now; a tiny lamb lying helpless alongside its dead mother was dispatched without breaking a step.

The exercise included recovering a wounded member of your patrol when in contact with the enemy, close quarter battle (*CQB*), moving along a twisting path, shooting at targets that popped up or those standing semi-concealed in cover, ambush drills, anti-ambush drills and so on. One lighter moment was to come on the night of a 'target reconnaissance' exercise. Boarding the old Bedford RL three-tonner, we hurtled along the South Wales roads. In the back, we rocked back and forth in the darkness of the battened down flap, waiting for the speed to drop off. Soon the lorry slowed to a stop, the tarp was lifted and the dark shape of the first man climbed out. A few stops later, it was my turn. The three-tonner roared into the darkness, leaving me in a cloud of diesel fumes. The tiny deserted road I had been dumped on was sky-lined above me and there were the dark brooding silhouettes of the Beacons. My mission was to find and produce a report on a railway tunnel entrance. My tiny covered torch illuminated the railway in its red glow to the north on the map but not as the elusive tunnel entrance!

Two hours later, my choices had been reduced to either hoofing it back to camp admitting failure or meeting the returning lorry with a cunning plan! I was chatting to the anonymous dark shadows of the other hopefuls as the three-tonner sped its way back, its differential whining in protest. A picture started to form and by the time we got back to camp, my report, gleaned from questioning the others, was a very credible likeness of a single-track railway running into the tunnel entrance and was deemed acceptable by the DS staff. Phew!

There was much more to learn of course, but this was for the future after a parachute course, getting 'badged' (*passing all the requirements*) and joining the squadron.

Escape and Evade!

We never did the evade and escape (*E&E*) as part of the continuation. But on arriving at the first 'drill' night, after arriving back from my parachute course, it was carried out. At least two squadron members grabbed me, a hood was crammed over my head and over the next couple of hours, I had a small taster of what interrogation techniques I might expect if captured.

At some point soon after some of us went down to the JSIU *(Joint Service Interrogation Unit)*, then based in Ashford, we submitted ourselves to be interrogated, and presumably gave the JSIU staff the opportunity to use their techniques. There were three groups who *had* to resist interrogation training: us, marines and aircrew. There may well have been others who worked on the 'dark side' too.

The weekend started with some lectures, what we might expect our captors to know. For instance, if you had been decorated, your name might well have been in print in some magazine or local paper, then there was every possibility that your interrogators would, shortly after your standard statement of "*Sorry, I can't answer that question, sir*", running your name rank and service number, research and soon know all about you and your family.

These techniques, along with sleep and sensory deprivation, being forced to hold stress positions, sometimes held outside day or night, possibly naked, all with hoods on and white noise in the background, were designed to break you down. We, for our part, were to try and resist for twenty-four hours, by which time the vast majority of what tactical information you knew would be redundant and of little value to the enemy.

At the end of the lectures, armed men came into the room and we were 'in the bag' the rest of the day, and night was very unpleasant. Between 'softening up', I was frog-marched in to face 'Mr Nasty' with bright lights in my eyes while he was shouting threats and obscenities at me. Or 'Mr Nice' offering a cigarette and trying to get a Red Cross statement signed so my family could be informed I was alive and well. By Sunday morning, when my hood was taken off and told it was all over, I wasn't sure if I believed it. Such was my confusion and it took some time before that distrust dissipated. Traveling back to Hitchin, all of us had a story to tell! We were all also well aware that what we had experienced was in the context of training. In the real thing, our experience might well be considerably worse, even before we got taken to an interrogation centre!

There was an occasion where this risk of 'going in the bag' was for real, which manifested itself later in nightmares that went on for some time after I left the regiment. They were all the same. I was in the bottom of a conical shell hole, helpless, and around the rim rode Russian Cossacks. Invariably at this point, Georgina would wake me, saying I was making loud unintelligible noises.

A major E&E came later when the whole regiment took part in an E&E exercise that winter. Stripped of our kit, we were herded onto old unheated railway carriages at Euston, guarded by soldiers in unfamiliar uniforms and armed with AK47s (*would this be allowed today I wonder?*). We were armed with only a 'sketch map' with north and a few landmarks on it. We were dumped unceremoniously and hungry onto the snow-covered freezing Stamford training area on one of the coldest nights for many years, our small party of three. Twins Pete and Dave looked for the pole star amongst the ice-cold clear twinkling night sky and set off. In the distance, we could see jeep headlights and troop transports stopping to drop off the hunter force.

Some time later, the situation had gone from an E&E exercise to one of survival! Looking at the others, with frozen snot on their top lips, frosted eyebrows and clothing white with frost, I could make out that things were getting serious!

We came upon a darkened farmhouse amongst the outbuildings an old abandoned and dilapidated caravan. Inside was our salvation, rolls and rolls of fiberglass insulation! It took no encouragement to wrap ourselves in them, knowing we are not going to freeze to death. The price was terrible itching when we finally emerged in the morning into a crystal-clear Sunday winter morning. As it happened, the exercise had been cancelled, the night-time temperature had been eighteen below, which had been deemed dangerously low even for us.

There were other E&E exercises, very often in Denmark, which went under the now politically incorrect name 'Black Maki'. These were double-edged in that the Dutch home

44

guards were put on alert; in fact, it seemed the whole country was on alert for our arrival. Entry was either by parachute, but more often on a low flying three-tonner *(lorry)* if the weather precluded jumping in.

We acted as Russian Spetsnaz tasked to attack various targets and then exfiltrate without being captured and falling into the clutches of the JSIU.

On one occasion, I was the only member who had not been captured when we were 'bumped' early one morning. I escaped with just my rifle and belt kit and made for the emergency RV, where the remainder of the squadron would be. Arriving without further incident, sitting down by a tree, it wasn't long before my teeth were chattering and my body was shaking with cold, trying to keep the frost off me. I had put my waterproof map over me as a sort of survival blanket.

Jim Shad offered to share his sleeping bag later, so we both had a very tightly squeezed but warm night. Jim says he can still remember how I smelt!

There was another night when we were waiting patiently out of the wind on the Dutch coast for a torpedo boat to pick us up. It had to hoof it as trucks started pulling up on the road; tails gates were banging down disgorging 'enemy' troops. I remember there was a lot of snow on the ground. We split up as we were outnumbered ten to one; we could fight, each of us to make for the emergency RV. Snow was very heavy on the ground, so it was impossible to hide your tracks. I remember walking backwards for some time in an attempt to confuse the hunters!

Another time and place, but the pictures tell the tale

On another ten-day NATO long-range patrol exercise 'Tristar', we had to face the hunter force; it was the third battalion of my old regiment, the Green Jackets. They had just come back from Ireland and were very sharp. They forced us to move frequently, as they cordoned off areas and carried out searches. In the end, the call was so close, we only just escaped with our weapons and belt kits, abandoning everything else and forced to live off our emergency rations until we could get to an agent RV. It was bitterly cold; finding somewhere as safe as we could, we tried resting, all four of us in the spoon position, taking it in turns to be in the middle!

In Northern Scotland, the country's last great wilderness.

Our task was to get across a mythical border into 'Blue' land (*friendly territory*) many miles south of our drop-off point. The *Gurkhas* were the hunter force; they have an enviable reputation, but as it turned out, they did not cause us a great deal of problems. The weather was very inclement, the rain driving them into whatever dry cover was available, allowing us the opportunity to slip by their 'stop lines' with very little hindrance. To this day on a rainy night, I say, "This is a good night for dirty deeds!"

Having to cross the (*I think*) River Spa to make for a boat to take us further south, Mick, who was lead scout was looking along the bank, in the dark of course for a crossing point, fell in! His voice growled back to us three tittering in darkness on the bank, "We're crossing here." One other incident came to mind later reading the 'Bravo 20' account of the first Gulf War when the half troop, who had been split up, stopped a taxi at gunpoint to get as far as they could towards the Jordanian border. Their bid failed as it happened at a checkpoint.

But for us, resting in cover one morning, we saw an ancient single-decker bus appear over the horizon, coming down towards us, on what was little more than a single-track road. Stepping out, we flagged it down. We were, by this time, filthy dirty, unkempt, unshaven and armed. The bus stopped and the driver asked with a twinkle in his eye, "How far are you going, boys?"

We said, "As far as possible please," and climbed in. Inside the door, to the left, was a wicker basket with some chickens in and on the first seat, there was a little lady dressed in black, clutching her shopping bag in her lap, who never batted an eyelid as the four of us barged past.

The ten miles or so ride we got was very welcome! I think the driver had done this before!

As you read on, I remind you that on each occasion, long or short, Georgina coped at home as many wives and partners did with whatever had to be coped with, routine or emergency, all without support and on each following Monday morning, us TA boys all went back to work!

Badged

"Stand up, hook up, check equipment," the PJI (*Parachute Jumping instructor)* shouted above the noise of the engines. Swaying and bracing myself, I latched my static line onto the overhead steel cable, checked my harness was all okay and ran my eye over the man's parachute pack in front of me. The Hercules was banking around towards the drop zone on Weston on the Green, pitching up and slowing. The PJI slid up the port para-trooping door. Immediately, cold gusty air rushed in from my position in the stick; the green Oxford countryside slid by below us. Levelling up, the red light on the doorframe came on. The PJI held up two fingers (*two minutes*); my legs were shaking. We shuffled forwards, the first man holding onto the doorframe. The red eye glared at us for what seemed ages and just as suddenly flicked to green. "GO! GO!" came the shout as the first man disappeared out of the door. Shuffling up in line, now it was me. Grabbing the doorframe and stepping out on the small ledge, I attempted to jump but my legs buckled and before I knew it, I was riding down the slipstream. The chute opened, I looked up to make sure it had deployed correctly, my hand on the reserve. The noise and drama inside the aircraft suddenly changed to peaceful silence as I swayed under my open green canopy.

Looking down onto the DZ (*drop zone*), those in front of me were now on the ground, their chutes collapsed like useless bundles of washing. Seconds later, my view changed as the green grass came rushing up. I bent my knees and turned my feet off to avoid toes, knees, nose and hospital, and to start my parachuting career. My feet banged down, knocking my breath away. Rolling forward, I stood up and it was all over. I had completed my first descent from an aircraft.

Parachutist!

This jump was to be the first of six, three from a balloon and three from an aircraft. This one had been clean fatigue (*without equipment*), the next was a two stick, jumping from alternative doors, followed by jumping with equipment in daylight and finally with equipment at night.

I had to get my weight from fourteen stone to thirteen and a half before I could go, joining the other four from 'C' Squadron, to report to RAF Abingdon, the No.1 parachute school, ten days previously.

For the first few days, training consisted of doing forward rolls onto matting, then jumping a few feet down from a mock up fuselage onto mats. Then, the controlled descents from a tower, followed by leaping from a mock-up exit door and sliding down a wire, the jump being followed by a short but dead drop, hence the name knacker cracker.

Moving onto the balloon for several descents was a strange experience: the cage with four of us in it was rising silently to eight hundred feet. Instinctively, you clutch the side to prevent you to fall out when you are about to jump out of the thing a few minutes later.

Our dispatcher called me to the opening – he was a comedian – and said, "If you pile in, can I have your boots?" followed by "GO". Again it is a dead drop but as you look up you can see your chute being pulled out of its bag and deploying. Then a disembowel voice from hundreds of feet below would say things like "Check your chute" or "Steer to the right" and as you approached the ground "Keep your feet together", all from the disembowelled megaphone voice of a PJI on the ground.

Adjusting kit fittings harness
Perlow Camp

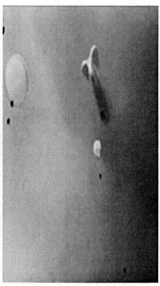

The Tower
Abingdon

The outdoor exit trainer

Becoming para-trained was the last requirement before becoming 'Badged'. SAS wings are different from normal para wings, in that they are upturned, in light blue, founded by David Stirling and then they are influenced by the design of the Egyptian 'Ba' bird symbol, bestowing the wearer with eternal flight after death.

They signified much more than that; the wearer was just para-trained but that also signified he had completed selection and continuation and was now a full-fledged member of a Sabre Squadron.

The parachute was one of the primary means of arriving at what was known as 'entry' (*getting into hostile territory*), but by no means the only one. Over my twelve and a bit year with the regiment, I did surprisingly few jumps. For instance, you only needed to do one a year to stay. That is all I did. Sometimes in the summer, we had a balloon or helicopter at RAF Henlow and could do three 'Hollywood' (*clean fatigue*) descents in the evening. Several jumps could take place as part of exercises in a year, both here and abroad. As well as jumping with the RAF, also jumping with the French 13th Parachutists du régiment (13RDP) and the US 11th Special Forces Group (11SFG), probably totalling about sixty descents give or take, in all. A small number of us were trained in HALO (*High Altitude Low Opening*) techniques for clandestine entry. I would have liked to have been part of that group, but it was not to be, as I was somewhere else at the time. Over the years, I had had the experience of jumping from a variety of aircraft, the C130 Hercules, various helicopters including off the tailgate of the Chinook, when it felt that you were about to step on the man's head in front of you, French Transal 140, an ancient C47 Dakota and US C123 Provider when on exchange with US special forces. The briefing was memorable, in that it was long and exhaustive. At the end, the guy on the stage was saying, "In the case of an emergency," when he suddenly stopped, looking at his pilot sat along the stage, saying, "What the hell do we do, in the case of an emergency?" We all laughed long and loud, but was he joking?

Jumping from a US Army Huey about 1980

Parachuting stories are legion. Like any bit of danger mild or great that has been shared, everyone has a story to tell. We jumped into water, small drop zones that caused landings in trees. As did my boss, Bill, who found out when jumping onto a very large DZ once but with a single lone tree in the middle of it. Someone walked across my canopy on one night jump, alarming the ground fellow squadron member, Alan, that it was very dangerous, who, thinking he saw a pond, released part of his harness in preparation of entering 'the water', then hit top of a convex-roofed building, sliding off and landing unceremoniously on the ground. The RAF dropped us early on one airfield exercise, some landing on the perimeter track; we had several injuries that day, with Squadron Sergeant Major Terry breaking both his ankles. I also broke an ankle later jumping in on a target attack exercise in Scotland, rescued by members of 'D' 23 SAS(V), spending the weekend being moved around Dundee in a wheelchair, very drunk and disorderly!

'Stand by, Stand bye', my artist impression of a night drop

Patrol Signaller

I was biting down hard on the pencil clamped in my teeth, concentrating on the faint Morse code coming from the finicky '301' receiver in my earpiece. I was scribbling down on my message pad the series of letters and numbers of the message 'base' was sending us. The signal was fading in and out with all sorts of radio chatter and music in the background from other transmitters across Europe. The ionosphere was also doing its evening thing of moving down and causing more problems. Terry, my patrol commander, crammed next to me in the narrow hollow just inside the tree line of the wood we were in, was watching and waiting for me to finish to find out the reply to the evening SITREP (*situation report*). Further along, the other two patrol members, Pete, our lead scout was scoffing a Mars bar, and Alan, our 'tail-end Charlie' was watching from under his camouflage face veil, the column of armoured vehicles of 'orange' (*exercise enemy*) forces growling and clanking by our position on the road below. Once the message was decoded, Terry got out his map and started studying it, then started to put down our reply. We both encoded and encrypted it using his codebook and my one-time pad (*each page only used once*). Now I was back on the 'net', this time on the '314' transmitter and started tapping our reply using the key fitted on its green rectangular corner, it's tiny four-and-half-watt signal going out from the aerial trailed along the overhead bushes to our base hundreds of miles to the West. "0A" (*base*), DE (*this is*) C 14 (*our patrol call sign*), "BT" (*long break*) followed by the "DTG" (*date time group*), then the groups of four numbers of the message, then "BT" (*long break again*) and finally "K" (*over*). Back came the acknowledgement QRK (*received and understood*). Ahead of us was the 'hard routine' snack food from the ration pack, and a long night's 'tab' (*tactical advance to battle*) to another location. Around us, there were, parked up camouflaged in by-roads and woods, dozens of vehicles and hundreds of 'Orange force' troops. We were deep in 'orange force' territory and will have to move with care.

Just after joining the squadron our OC (*officer commanding*), Kevin, decided that everyone should be able to signal, given our traditional role at the time of raiding and reconnaissance. It was a very important aspect of the patrols cross training. To this end, for some time, our 'drill' nights were taken up in the signals' room at Hitchin under the watchful eye of Bud and Russ, two of our senior signallers. We sat at the long-partitioned bench, Morse keys in hand, earphones on, trying to learn this strange language of dots and dashes. What transpired was that some of us started to get on well, others not so and some could not get the hang of it at all and never would. Being one that could, along with other promising candidates, I was put on a signals' course destined to become a patrol signaller.

The course was held in London at our Duke of York's HQ. So once a month, I found myself travelling down to do much the same as we were doing on the squadron drill nights. Towards the end, however, I was going out on the South Downs to practice our burgeoning skills outside. Also, driving to work or sitting reading a book would often try to spell out the words and numbers in Morse in my head.

We also could take home a '128' set for 'home working'. The '128' was an old wartime radio built into a suitcase and used by SOE agents (*special operations executives*). It used crystals and could be powered by battery or mains electricity. When at home, we very often would take a picnic out with our young son to a country park. Once settled, we connected the 'set' to the car battery, so it was 'working' (*transmitting and receiving*) back to the London base, often to the puzzled looks of passers-by. At home, the aerial trailed out the window and the set was plugged into a light socket. I found it interfered with the TV, and probably with our neighbour's set as well. I soon became more proficient and learnt the mnemonics of the Morse rather than the dots and dashes. The letter 'F', for instance, comes through as 'did it hurt you', and 'Q' as 'here comes the bride'. Developing my 'fist' in time meant other operators could tell who was on the other end of the transmission. I was starting to get cocky and started sending codes faster all the time, until 'base' sent back a message even faster, forcing me to send 'QSL' (*Please send more slowly*). Lesson learned!

That year, the regiment went to Barrage in the French Alps for its 'camp' accompanied by French Alpine instructors, to learn the skills of climbing and operating in mountainous terrain. But this was not for me, finding myself in a French army base in Ger, a small garrison town further north. There, during our days, and sometimes evenings, we continued to practice Morse and 'Q' codes (*each code meaning something*). One evening, needing some fresh air before the next class, I found myself in a cafe near the main gate. By that time, I was starting to learn a few very basic French words and could order a beer. The barmaid, a mature and well-rounded lady in her forties, giving me my beer, smiled and said something in French. I could do nothing more than politely smile back, a French soldier further along the bar, giving me a huge grin, translated, saying, "She said you are a beautiful English soldier." Not wanting to be another notch on her pump handles, I smiled politely, looked at my watch, finished my beer and exited smartly!

Still new, look at that beret!

Very often, we would go up into the foothills, with our expert Joe from the regular regiment's signals' squadron, both to get a bit of exercise and also practice setting up and 'working' back to the base now in Ger. I don't ever remember doing it at night or in inclement weather.

The joys of lying under a poncho at night, rain pattering on the outside, my tiny red light held in my teeth was yet to come!

Signals' course France early 1972

At the end of this period, I was honoured that our then Squadron Sergeant Major Terry chose me to be his signaller, a partnership that was to last several years.

Cyprus

Kitted up and briefed, we were ready to go. The only way was up as our 'Boss', Kevin, had set up the squadron headquarters on one of the highest points in the northeast of the island for the three-day exercise in the mountains. Just as we were about to leave the, '2ic' (*second in command)* rushed over with a signal saying, "The boss needs water." We looked with dismay at the five-gallon jerry can in his other hand. A gallon of water weighs ten pounds, so this was going to weigh fifty pounds give or take a bit and this was on top of the sixty odd we already were carrying; we were not impressed. Being a new boy out for the first time with my adopted patrol, it was a case of gritting my teeth and getting on with it. During the next hour, we took it in turns to carry the can (*how true was that old saying*). Arriving hot and sweaty, the can was promptly taken from us and out of the corner of my eye, I saw the boss was filling his mess tin so he could have a shave. Terry, my PC (*patrol commander),* said nothing and raised an eyebrow; rank has its privileges as I had just experienced.

Cyprus was my first camp after joining the squadron; over the next ten days or so, I was learning a great deal about the basics of patrol life and its routines. In many respects looking back, the whole regiment did mainly all the basic activities and, thus, Cyprus slipped into the following years as an unmemorable time.

We used the ranges several times, zeroing our weapons. We cheated on a shooting competition with our sister 'D' squadron while taking our turn in the butts (shooting *range*). We brought down the figure to eleven targets and were pasting over their bullet holes before they walked up to count them, and thus 'C' squadron had the winning score! We trained with the Royal Corps of Transport landing craft, with whom bizarrely we could not communicate with, as we only used Morse code at the time,

There was quite a lot of down time, as men were falling out of the morning muster parade as sickness and diarrhoea swept through our ranks. Mick and I found ourselves in a cellar bar one evening having a beer, when four Cypriot guys came in with two sitting at each side of us, trapping us in. My heart rate rose dramatically, as this looked like big trouble. Pretending to continue chatting, Mick said under his breath, "You take two on the right, I'll hand the others."

This standoff lasted a few more minutes when just as quickly they upped and left, followed very shortly by us. We also had the opportunity to go down to the shore after our three-day exercise. We were swimming in the sea and playing 'Pyramids and Bombing', where the player holding a pebble between his bare cheeks waddled forward to try and release it onto the target in the sand. When it was Terry's turn, his 'bomb' would not release, as it turned out to be a lump of congealed oil. So we had to hold him down and clean it out with sand! A story that still stands the test of time at reunions.

Posing with my first patrol: Terry, Pete and Alan

White Bison

It was nearly the last light on the fourth day. I was starving hungry; the few filthy potatoes we had dug up and boiled two nights ago were a distant memory. Hearing the approaching engine of a light aircraft, I looked at the others; they obviously had heard it too. Needing no encouragement from Dave, our patrol commander took cover; an on-exercise aircraft could either be friend or foe. The little aircraft flew over us a few minutes later. Taking a chance, Dave signalled. It was a Belgium Air Force Auster, banking around to circle back over us, the crewman threw out what proved to be a large ration pack.

My artist impression was painted years later.

Needless to say, our next meal was fit for a king! The ration pack meal proved to be American. To our amusement, it contained a packet of French letters. We thought the likelihood of us putting them to good use was to say the least unlikely. We were going to be using them over the muzzles of our rifles to keep them clean. There was also chewing gum and five cigarettes, none of which were ever in our own issue rat-packs (*ration packs*).

Two days previously, about a dozen of us from 21 and 23 SAS(V) stood in a little clearing alongside the massive Ardennes Forest, on the German-Belgium border.

The Belgium paratroopers, part of the hunter force, were watching as we were being searched prior to the start of a week's E&E, all part of the annual NATO exercise, Eugenie.

The Belgians searched through every bit of kit, then us being ordered to undress, they went over our clothes as well, relieving us of anything we could eat, smoke or spend. Managing to secrete an Oxo cube where the sun didn't shine, I had a smug but uncomfortable feeling in my nether regions, when we were finally released and got under way.

Our mission was to get to an RV across a national border in 'blue' (*friendly*) territory to the east. The next night, using the cube to flavour the potatoes we had dug up, we boiled them; nobody noticed, as it was no longer square! The potatoes, covered in soil, made for a gritty but gratefully received meal.

The following day proved to be uneventful as we made our way east. The exercise area was massive, so we knew that the hunter forces had their work cut out to capture us. Their tactic, we surmised, would be to ambush probable 'choke' points that the necessity for speed and the terrain would channel us evaders into. On the evening of the second night, just as the light was beginning to fade, we found ourselves walking along a narrow track with a steep fall on one side and banked wood on the other. Ahead forty yards up, the track disappeared into the blackness of the mouth of the forest. Being lead scout, my mind said it was a possible ambush site for the hunter force. Signalling the others to stop, I whispered, to my 'boss', my concerns about the threatening entrance into the wood. Dave nevertheless ordered me forward to investigate. Thinking, *Thanks Dave*, I started forward, weapon at the ready, although none of us had any ammunition up the track. Approaching the blackness of the entrance, hearing what sounded to my nervous ear like the distinctive click of a safety catch, I turned on my heels and ran flat out back down the track.

To the amazement of the rest of the patrol kneeling in cover at the trackside, I went thundering past! I don't remember seeing them, such was my haste, only coming to a stop when out of breath. Several minutes later, sheepishly walking back to the rest of them, I saw their teeth white in the darkness as they grinned at my antics. As it happened, there was no ambush or more dramas that night or the following days. Some time later that night, however, we managed to get separated from our tail-end Charlie, Jim. Losing contact is surprisingly easy when moving in the near blackness of a forest at night, something that was to happen to me many years later in America. We didn't see Jim again until meeting in the safety of the final RV at the end of the exercise. 'Eugenie' was my first patrol after joining the squadron. This set the scene for many years to come, taking part in exercises each year in addition to the one annual 'camp'.

There was another 'Eugenie' several years later, but this time, I participated as a sergeant and patrol commander. We joined special forces from right across NATO, Spanish mountain commandos, who wore the berets at a rakish angle and large daggers on their belts, and French troops from the 13th Regiment Dragoons Parachutists. These were also our hosts. Using French aircraft, we were dropped in small groups all across the very rugged 'Massif Central'.

Our mission was to 'recce' bridges to see if they would stand the use of heavy armour (*tanks*). We were reporting back by long distance communication to the French para base, before exfiltrating across the very rugged 'Massif' to an LZ (*landing zone)* to be picked up by a French helicopter. French marine infantry was the 'enemy' hunter force.

Things went wrong from day…or rather night one. The French dropped into a very tight DZ, sloped with a tree that Mac, our fourth member, managed to land in. On top of this, our Greek signaller, 'George', on loan from 'A' Squadron, somehow managed to jettison his Bergen on the way down, finally finding it and all its contents complete with the rifle strapped on the outside smashed to bits. Even the zip on his sleeping bag was broken. The radio, of course, was rattling like a moneybox, completely useless.

We had an emergency RV where a French agent could be contacted should we need one. Obviously, we did and on the following night, we made the RV inside the time window; the agent would be waiting. Agent contacts are, as you would expect, very dodgy things to do, having no idea if it is compromised or not. We took the necessary precautions of observing the contact location before our agent arrived. Barry, our lead scout, and I approached him on high alert. We had a password to assure him that we also had not been compromised, in this case, 'White Bison'. The procedure using a password is that the challenge is made with the first part of the password and the reply should be the second part. Our agent decided not only to use both parts of the password but to add to our confusion, saying (*obviously*!), "Bison blanc," in French. The pregnant pause that followed seemed to go on forever, before our Anglo-Saxon brains realised what had been spoken to us numkins, who had not realized we would be spoken to in French.

Contact was made. A radio, essential to our mission and the bare necessities of life for George to continue was collected. On approaching 'our' bridge the following night, in the darkness, we were being followed by a herd of cows, each it seemed had a bell around its neck. Fortunately, the bridge was not guarded so we were able to do the recce, making contact the following day to send our report on the morning SITREP *(situation report)*.

Several years had passed since my first experience of possible ambush sites. I had forgotten the principles that in rugged or closed countries, the 'enemy' were likely to ambush any pinch points.

The result was that the following night, I walked straight into one. In exercise, the 'game' is up in this situation. For real, no doubt there would have been an exchange of fire; that, I fear, we would have come out of very badly indeed. Underlining why armies exercise: for failing to prepare is preparing to fail.

The French marines relieved us of our weapons and equipment. Expecting rough treatment, a bag over the head and zip-tied hands, we were surprised that they only ushered us into their truck. With both us and the marines in the back, we set off, with the unpleasantness in the interrogation centre still on my mind. Seats on foreign troop trucks very often faced out. For the first several minutes, trying to summon the courage to simply dive out into the night, I failed miserably.

We arrived back at what looked like the upstairs hayloft amongst some farm buildings. To our amazement, we were shown to a row of camp beds amongst our captors! It was a plan that although we certainly had been captured, we were now being treated as guests. The following morning, we were transported back to the same site and released.

Relieved and slightly bemused by the turn of events that went on our way, eventually after cross graining some very rugged country, we made the RV and our lift, a French Air Force Puma came into view, low over the trees, banking and landing with typical Gaelic flair. Half an hour later, we were deposited back to the 13 RDP base. We found some of our other patrols were back. We were sharing half our billet with the Spanish mountain commandos, who had amazingly been withdrawn because it was too wet!

Our last night in the barracks was riotous, coming back from the debrief in the main building, where the French colonel told his assembled regiment that the Brits had walked over a hundred kilometres in three days and two nights. Not only that, they were reservists. Hundreds of heads turned to see who these dozen men were with beige berets standing quietly along the back wall. Back in our billet, the Spaniards were amazed when we brought back beers from the canteen and then started playing the mad game of 'flaming arseholes'. Each competitor was clamping a rolled-up page of newspaper between his bare cheeks, and it was then set on fire. The object being to get to the other end of the barracks and back before the flame reached his nether regions.

I expect Spaniards veterans are still telling the story today as I am.

"Do You Speak English?"

Stumbling out of the noisy, laughter-filled guesthouse, expecting to see our transport waiting for us, we were greeted with nothing but deserted street lamps marching off into the darkness. Someone went back in, the noise and light washing over us as the door opened and closed, tempting us with another beer, returned to say that with the help of some and gesticulating, the landlord had done the necessary and a taxi was on its way. Any off-duty time generally amounted to one night in the local town the night before we departed. Transport known to all as the 'Passion Wagon' was organised by RHQ (*Regimental Headquarters*). This left at 19:30 on the dot, dropping us in the town centre. Later, the one and only pick up back to camp left at 23:00 and on this occasion, we had missed it. The taxi arriving very shortly; the universal cab, a bog-standard Mercedes, was well used to taking inebriated squaddies back to their camp and needed no instructions. Once the three of us had crammed in the back seat, our leader, Terry, sitting in the front decided he wanted a cigarette. A lot of us had the fifthly habit of smoking back then, but no one had a light so he then attempted to negotiate with the driver, who spoke as much English as Terry did German, and asked in a drunken slur and his best pigeon German. "You um smokum?" The driver, not surprisingly, had no idea what he was talking about, and Terry repeating the ridiculous phrase in a louder voice did not get our smokes lit nor improve the British-German relations!

At least once a year, the SAS(V) regiment found itself in Germany, taking part in a major exercise. The British Army stood toe to toe with the very nasty looking 13th Shock Army part of the GSFG (*Group of Soviet Forces Germany*). We were involved in either training for our primary role or, very often, acting as part of 'enemy orange forces', Russian Spetsnaz.

'C' Sqn, Friend or Enemy

All squaddies pick up some basic local language wherever they were in the world and we were no exception. On our visits to BAOR, we learned to order curried sausage with some chips (*Currywurst mit ein paar frits*), some beer (*ein große Biere bitte*) and for the Romeos amongst us, "How much for all night?" (*Wie viel für die ganze Nacht?*) But when it came to anything more, things became a bit more of a challenge.

It was common at the time for the regiments' soldiers to go on language courses for Arabic when deployed in North Africa, Aden and Yemen in the early years, along with the Malaysian emergency and the 'confrontation' in Borneo later and so on. But once NI (*Northern Ireland*) raised its ugly head, all eyes were, for a long time, focused across the Irish Sea. As a result of these ongoing diversions, learning to speak German took a back seat!

But as our main area of interest was in Germany, RHQ thought that we really should learn some useful German phrases. With the 'Poison Dwarf' (AKA Kevin) some months later trying to locate a German army barracks, where the Regiments 'Quick Move' kit was stored, we were soon lost in the maze of streets and buildings of the huge conurbation that is the Ruhr Valley. We stopped to try out our newly learned phrases on an elderly gentleman sitting out on his doorstep. I was driving at the time and watched KW walk back to the old guy and ask in his best German, "*Good* afternoon, sir, could you direct me to the local army barracks please?" ("*Guten Tag, können Sie direkt uns zu den Kasernen bitte.*") Watching in the wing mirror, the old boy jumped up, his eyes lit up and he took his pipe out to gesticulate. He began with much arm waving to give instructions to our missing destination.

The display went on for several minutes, and finally with a wave of thanks, KW returned. Jumping into the passenger seat, the look on his face said it all. "Well, I asked, which way? I have not got a f****ing clue," came the retort. The old German thought the fluently presented question clearly indicated that the enquirer also understood fluent German, and he had replied in kind and at speed in his native tongue! A fatal flaw had been revealed in our cunning plan! Later after we had located our gear, the crack widened! We decided with a couple of hours to spare, we would find the nearest guesthouse and have a bite to eat. As I quite fancied my own skills in the language department, I insisted on ordering our meal; the waiter took our order for a couple of large beers (*zwei große Biere bitte*), then with a slightly puzzled air, dutifully wrote down what was ordered to eat walking away with a slight shake of his head.

We sat and sipped our beers. About twenty minutes later, he reappeared with our meals, consisting of boiled potatoes, mashed potatoes and chips! We decided at that point that the only phrase we need was *"Sprechen Sie Englisch?"* (*Do you speak English?*)

My artistic impression of a night pick up, painted some years later

Going Commando

In the mid-1970s, I found myself on the list to go on a jungle course in far-flung Malaya with our regular sister 'D' Sqn 22 SAS. But first, having to get some jabs organised, I called the Pioneer Corps, who in the 1970s had a barracks in nearby Northampton, the nearest place I could go for my malaria, typhoid and other nasties. The MO *(medical officer)* could see me next Saturday morning. Now as it happened in those far-flung days of my married life, we very often went to or held a house party; this Saturday was no exception. The party was to be a fancy dress at a nearby neighbour's house, the theme was the orient. Duly going along the next Saturday and seeking out the MO, or to be precise his nurse, I encountered a well built and very capable looking lady, who was going to administer the jabs. She said with a stern warning that under no circumstances was I to have any alcohol. Now at the time, I reckoned I was a good example of a twenty-four-year-old prime British beef and was not inclined to be told what to do by an overbearing lady. Back home in the early evening, up in the master bedroom, I donned my Charlie Chang outfit, complete with droopy moustache and a long-plaited pigtail. Of course, this was accompanied with a small dram of the golden liquid. A little

76

later having become aware of the lack of movement from upstairs, Georgina came to investigate and found me, hat, pigtails and Charlie Chan moustache slewed to one side, sparko on the bed. Loving me as she did at the time, she subdued her giggles in case I was awakened and gently pulled the covers over me for the remainder of the evening and indeed the night! On Sunday awaking slightly bemused at my attire and situation, but feeling basically okay, it was time to complete my packing.

I only really heard of Malaya from Britain's ten-year involvement in defeating the Communist threat in the 1950s.

However, I did know that it was going to be hot and humid, but did not know of course just how hot and humid! Aware that some of the things you did not do in the jungle were your everyday activities of bathing, shaving and dabbing on a little Old Spice or changing one's underwear from time to time or putting one's jimjams on at night.

I expected to be away from home for about three months, six weeks of these would be 'upcountry' in the boondocks (*jungle*), learning how to live and fight in the jungle. So hygiene really came to the fore; there would be no use of soap or shaving cream and the like, and certainly no deodorant as all these would be a dead give-away to anyone who lived or moved about there. To this end, I put my fertile mind to the problem of underwear, because one only carried two sets of clothes, jungle fatigues, worn in the day and one of OGs to change into at night to sleep in. On the market, there had come some throwaway men's (*and presumably ladies and "other ranks"*) underwear; this was made of some sort of rayon, the nearest I can think of today would be throwaway Jey clothes. I thought these would do admirably, as I could simply take off the grungy ones and put on new from the estimated six needed for the six weeks (*or possible three if I put them on inside out for a week*), once in the boondocks. They also had the advantage of being very flimsy and light and as one had to carry whatever you needed, these throwaway knickers sounded just the ticket. But going back to having recovered from the weekend's activities, I kissed my beloved goodbye, picked up my assorted kit complete with new underpants and was on my way to Brize Norton to start my attachment. Arriving and reporting, I found myself along with three others, one from 'D' Sqn '21' and two from 'R' Sqn '22' (*the regulars own reserve squadron*), who were to become my patrol. We were with about sixty others all boarding the aircraft with its backward facing seats used in the RAFs troopers in those days.

With much revving of engines and vibrations as the pilot held the overladen aircraft against its brakes, we set off first heading for Cyprus and arrived there after dark some six hours later. This was my first experience of the near east, and stepping off from the crowded and hot cramped interior of the 'Brit' into the lovely cool and star-studded Cypriot night was like stepping into Peter Pan's Never-never-land. To cap it all, we were astonished to be fed in the RAF mess complete with white tablecloths and waiters!

After just an hour, we were back on the plane heading across the Med, down the Nile Delta and out into the Indian Ocean heading for Gan, a tiny dot of rock at that time, a vital fuelling stop for transiting RAF aircraft.

This proved to be a dusty fly-ridden airstrip with a corrugated tin shed at one end of the runway. Disembarking, we stood bleary eyed and now slightly dishevelled, waiting, in the early morning coolness of the Arabian dawn, while an ancient fuel bowser trundled up from some far-flung buildings and refuelled us for the next leg, Singapore.

Later that day out of the tiny window of the 'Brit', I caught my first sight of the little island that held the Singapore City. It was the causeway across to Lahore and then the vastness of the jungle extending as far as the eye could see. The aircraft circled and with a rumble of lowering undercarriage and whine of the flaps being extended, it alighted smoothly on the tarmac of RAF Changi. Getting off the plane, thinking at first that the engines were still running and we were walking through the hot exhaust gases, it was only when I cleared the wing tip that I realised this was the normal late afternoon tropical temperature. The humidity was such that within a dozen paces, my shirt was stuck to my back, and ominously my underpants to my parts where the sun does not shine. Having got our kit, we heaved it onto waiting lorries and, sweating heavily, boarded the hot and humid waiting buses to head for Nee Soon Barracks. There was a night's tossing and turning on army camp beds before sorting out what we had to take and what was going into storage. My kit was soon piled up and stuffed into my Bergen rucksack, including, of course, now only five pairs of my dainty blue throwaway knickers.

By midday, I found myself to be Number 4 in a 'stick' of eight men waiting for the next lift from the RAF Wessex helicopters that had been assigned to lift us up to base camp some eighty miles up country. With a huge down wash of rotor blades, the chopper settled on the grass. The Martian-like figure of the crewman waved us forward to mount the aircraft.

We chucked our kit aboard and scrambled in. With a glance out of the door, I the crewman reporting to the pilot over his radio, his voice lost in the hammering of the engines and whirling rotor blades, that everyone was aboard. We lifted off, wheeling out and heading north towards the waiting jungle. With the door open, the cool air washed into the helicopter as first the barracks, then houses and roads slipped past beneath us to be replaced by occasional dirt-logging road, then the solid green mat of the jungle. Thirty minutes later, the engine note changed as the aircraft banked, wheeled and descended. Another logging track came into view with a river and a bridge. A few minutes later, the Wessex settled onto the middle of the bridge and we jumped off. The Martian heaved off our rucksacks, some rations and a couple of boxes of ammo and without more ado, the aircraft left in a swirl of dust and small stones, disappearing within seconds. The heat was also back within seconds. I was holding my weapon in one hand and heaved my rucksack onto my shoulder, sweat popping out from every pore with every movement. It was about a mile up the logging track from the helipad. Then off into the ulu *(jungle)* and down towards the base camp alongside the Songy *(rive*r*)* Bong. The move lasted about three quarters of an hour before we arrived at the place that was going to be home for some time to come, but all was not well and things didn't feel right 'down below'. After the introduction briefing from the DS, taking the chance to slip away and inspect the reason for the strange sensations under my fatigues, it was soon revealed. All that was left of my modern man disposables were three strips of elastic, one around each leg and one around my waist. It looked like I was going commando for the next six weeks.

Food and Kampong   *Hearts and minds' visit*

"Where the hell have those blokes been?" I said, peering out through the thick 'atap' *(thorny bushes)* we had spent the night in. The total blackness was starting to turn to grey, and something caught my eye. Was that a man standing alongside the nearest tree, or was it an animal? Surely not a horse? Or could it be? We were a dozen miles from any habitation. My heart had suddenly gone from sleepy rest to thumping so loud that the man or horse or whatever it was would be able to hear it. I had to make a decision to either wake the patrol now or wait. The seconds tick by; my mouth had gone dry as the grey of dawn slowly but surely turned to daylight. What had looked like a man, or horse and rider, turns into just another jungle fond. *What a 'dip stick,'* I think to myself; that was a close call.

The last stag *(on watch)* was normally the quiet one. The chorus of birds and insects making their myriad of chirps and buzzes had yet to start.

It was where the saying "You can't see the hand in front of your face" was really true. The brain can easily be taken over by imagination and easily fooled, as it had just happened to me.

One of 'C' Squadrons patrols, Pete, had mistaken the luminous dials of his watch and read upside down, as watches were hung from a cord around the neck, as twelve thirty at night instead of six in the morning. Waking the patrol as ordered for its early start. He was not in the flavour of the day!

For those who have not had the pleasure of the jungle, devices for night-time viewing were still in their infancy. So when darkness fell at 1900 on the dot, it was almost impossible to move about, except perhaps along a track of some sort. So on patrol, the late afternoon routine was moving off the line of march and setting up the '316' radio to send the afternoon SITREP *(situation report on the day's activities and getting new orders)*. Then, move on for an hour or so doing some minor tactics that included a U-turn to make sure there was no following up.

All before finding some very thick and spiky 'atap' bushes, getting in the middle for the night's LUP *(lying up position)*. It was only then that the evening routine could start, of each, in turn, cleaning weapons, get some 'scof', rig a basha with a hammock and make ready a parachute sleeping bag. Then stand too *(be on guard)*, all before the blackness descended. Each member then did a turn at 'stag' *(on watch)* throughout the night.

Both signaller and patrol commander

It was on day seven of a week of uneventful patrol. The only exception was a brief period of excitement while watching, from the jungle, a young Chinese woman doing her morning *Tai Chi* exercises on their long house veranda. As well as doing square searches, being part of our brief, we also did heart and mind visits to local villages, where on one occasion, we gave the headman's wife, who had been ill for several days, half an aspirin. Within a few minutes, she was up and obviously feeling a lot better, such was the power of simple medication on her drug-free body. We also gave some of our precious boiled sweets to the kids for whom they must have been a great treat. They would grab them and run away, laughing and chattering. Our toilet paper was also in demand, not to be used for its purpose but for writing on when needed.

By way of a thank you, the family invited us to eat, gave us what looked like pre-chewed nuts or something on a banana leaf. I was smiling my thanks and swallowing each mouthful as fast as possible!

Of course our visits were double-edged as Danny, our linguist, chatted to the family and gleaned any useful information on what was going on in the area.

Giving away some of my precious boiled sweets and 'bog' paper required a special sort of determination not to eat or use them because everything had to be carried and this could be a tricky balancing act, as there was only so much that could be crammed in a Bergen and belt kit.

The list could be endless: ammo, radio, code books, batteries, dry clothing and plimsolls for sleeping in, hammock, parachute sleeping bag, medic pack, compass, *gollock* (*machete*), some PE *(plastic explosive)* and the paraphernalia that goes with it. Spare batteries, the list goes on. Not forgetting food and water! The bulky ration packs were pared to the bone. Breakfast, a brew and maybe sardines on the hard-tack biscuits. Midday, something quick and easy like a Mars bar. Night-time may be a sweet curry for me, always carrying curry paste, along with rice if it had not been used in a 'rice' pudding. The remainder was buried!

Coming to the end of the patrol, food was running out, as we had eaten more than we thought we needed. We decided to head back to our buried treasure. Approaching with caution and observing the site, three of us took up kneeling defensive positions as the lead scout went forward in 'light order' (*without his Bergen*). He stopped in the small clearing and started to clear away the jungle debris. Seeing the first glint of the ration pack wrapper, he turned and grinned back to me; his teeth startling white against his grizzled bearded face. Food!

The next day, we waited for the thumping of the New Zealand helicopter coming to fetch us. We throwing out the agreed colour smoke grenade, and the aircraft appeared into view over the jungle canopy setting down on our logging track landing pad. We needed no second bidding from the Martian-like crewmen's becking hand to run forward at the crouch. We chuck our Bergens on board, clambering in the Huey (*US made helicopter*). The engine note rose, we lifted off. As the cool air washed over us like some summer shower, I looked around at the others; they looked exhausted. Everyone was unshaven, and their clothes were on the point of disintegration. Not long after, the mattress of jungle changed to the odd track, then the road and finally the outskirts of the Nee-soon Barracks.

The Huey banked, flared and settled down on the camp grass. Without ceremony, we jumped out of the aircraft; it immediately lifted off and departed. The light after the gloom of the jungle was starting, and to my surprise, it was Sunday morning. The quartermaster, as was the custom, had lit a petrol fire to burn our tattered clothing. Once done, we picked up our kit and weapons and started making our way back to our basha.

Being Sunday, the ANZAC (*Australian and New Zealand*) troops were on parade; they looked, out of the corner of my eye, immaculate as we traipsed past clad, only in skivvies and boots.

One of them was heard saying, "Blimey, where have those blokes been?"

A sketch drawn much later as part of a publication in our association magazine

Down Under

The distance from Nee-Soon Barracks gate down to the main road was a short one; on either side, local traders had set up their stalls, you could buy just about anything. Off duty servicemen, of which there were many, were forced to walk past each time they entered or left. Needless to say, each stallholder would harass you on each passing. Having done our time in the jungle, we had three days off. In those few days, my spare uniform had been cleaned and pressed by 'SoSo', a tiny wizened lady that seemed to have free range around the camp and took in washing and repairs. All my clothes, even my disgusting blue underpants, unashamedly put in had come back a mottled grey, all delivered immaculately pressed and folded for just a couple of dollars.

One of the nicest experiences had been a visit to the botanical gardens, walking amongst the stunning flora and fauna in quiet solitude. Georgina and I visited again many years later in my ship-refurbishment days to enjoy its magnificent displays.

I was wanting, however, to buy a small camera and stopped on one of my forays into town at a stall crammed with all sorts of watches and cameras. I was immediately being set upon by the owner. "You wanna buy one? I give you a good price," he said, coming forward when he saw my interest. Being a new boy and having been warned not to accept the first or even the second price, I waved him off, walking away to his pleas until out of earshot, by which time, of course, the next stallholder had taken over. On day three and my last walk out, the price had come sufficiently to what seemed reasonable, and I bought one.

The last night was a sort of right of passage for the regiment's soldiers visiting Singapore, a visit to 'Boogie Street'. During the day, the Boogie, real name Bugis, was an insignificant narrow street with shops, bars and stalls, as many others were in the city.

At night, however, the stalls disappeared, and tables and chairs came out into the road. Music started to play as people started to arrive and the evening got going. Our merry band was no exception. Ordering beers, we took a table and waited for the main event, the appearance of the local *Ki-ties*. These transgender people came looking for 'business'; us squaddies were, of course, prime targets!

The 'ladies' were not shy; one making a beeline for us, sat on my lap saying, "You want good time, soldier boy, only twenty dollars?"

Someone in the background caught my eye, getting ready to take a photograph. Putting my hand up, I shouted, "No, don't! My wife is never going to believe this is a bloke!"

Even up close, 'she' looked stunning. Embarrassed and laughing, I pushed 'her' off. 'She' came back twice as the night wore on, the price lowered first to twelve dollars and finally for free!

I will leave it up to the reader's imagination as to what 'good time' involved, but it was never going to be good enough for me.

We did hear of one of our squadron lads, who did take up an offer, then went missing for two days. He came back wearing a big smile, saying he had been well fed and 'looked after'. The only thing that worried him was 'her' flat had two locks on it, one to get in and one to get out!

The following evening bused down to Changi Airport. There was an hour or so to wait before boarding the RAF Britannia. I was wandering about the airport's spacious marble-covered shopping area and stopped to look in the window of a camera shop. There displayed was my camera and it was cheaper! The stallholder had seen me coming in the end.

That evening, we were on our way, looking out the window as the lights of Singapore slipped behind us. Ahead were the dark night skies as we headed south across Indonesia and the Coral Sea towards Darwin, Australia.

The next day, our hours break in the bar at Darwin Airport was suddenly interrupted in true Australian style, by a white-boiler-suited man coming in and shouting above the hubbub, "They are ready to go if you are."

Serviced, we were once again on our way. This time across the vast wilderness that is the Australian outback, the Tasmanian Sea to our next stop, Auckland, New Zealand, to meet their SAS Squadron.

Our visit was the first time that the two countries' regiments had met since Korea. I'm not sure if it was on a significant date or not, but it was as the navy would say 'showing the flag', a mixture of socialising, cross training and exchanging experiences as the Kiwis had been on operations in the Vietnam War. We finally finished up at a place called Wangaupura and received a welcoming speech from their squadron's 'boss'. Pretty well, the next day got down to an introduction to tracking by a colour blind Maori. He was very impressive. Tracking is a skill that can be taught but has to be practiced and, therefore, we were never going to excel.

This was part of an unremarkable exercise of several days. One night, while lying in my sleeping bag, I was listening to the huge storm outside, which was bringing rotten trees crashing down around us in the forest; I was hoping our number was not up. My own excitement was a wild sow bore running straight through the two-man 'basha' being shared with 'Horse', an 'R' Squadron guy, followed by six squealing youngsters.

We had a week or so having the choice of activities from the New Zealanders. Not wanting to do anything, I took a few days out living on the 'Thousand Island Beach', swimming in the day and sleeping under the stars at night. Others did rock climbing, abseiling, shooting deer from helicopters or parachuting from their ancient WWII Dakota aircraft. On the last day, I elected to join in, standing in the door, waiting for the green light. The doorframe, worn away to its bright alloy skin by a thousand hands and the many layers of paint, told the tale of the aircraft's long life.

We were free most evenings and were not giving it a great deal of thought at the time, because we had been our own TA patrol in Malaya and we had very little to do with the remainder of the squadron. We found ourselves pretty much the same in New Zealand. We never, for instance, went to any combined social events, of which there must have been several. In fact, the regulars were conspicuous by their absence.

Only one guy talked to me on a regular basis, the only others who did to any degree were from our accompanying 264 (SAS) signals' squadron.

We were kept at an arm's length. The locals, however, could not have been more welcoming. While having a beer on my own one evening in the local Returned Servicemen's Club, their equivalent to our British Legion, I was invited to join a couple of locals on a nearby table. One offered me the keys to his house as he was away for a few days, saying, "Just put it under the doormat when you have finished." On another occasion, I got an invite to go back for Sunday dinner and the use of the family's natural hot tub. This was gratefully accepted and I had a very pleasant afternoon of family life when so far away from my own. This has left me with a very fond memory of our Kiwi cousins that has lasted to this day.

On the very last day, all of us and the Kiwi guys, along with their families, filled the then small airport. One guy had brought a guitar and before long the whole place was rocking with great wartime songs like 'We will meet again'. It was followed by a very emotional goodbye their 'boss' coming on the aircraft shaking hands with every one of us.

Our journey home had two stops, both out of necessity and the need to catch up with events in the Middle East. We stopped first on a small island base of the Omani coast. Here, 'D' squadron went off for a briefing on the current situation. We were pointedly excluded. We understood that the ethos of 'need to know' applied, but nevertheless, we felt very much what the regulars thought of us, being firmly put in our place as very second-class soldiers. Then, we were off again onto Cyprus and finally RAF Lynham. We were descending through the clouds to a rainy England and I was looking forward very much to seeing my family again. But the rain also reminded me that we were back in Europe; this was just as well, because a couple of months later, I was in, what NATO called its northern flank, Norway and just in time for my daughter Chloe to be born.

The Northern Flank

Looking down from the bus windows at the tiny twinkling lights of Rjukan in the valley below, I hoped the driver knew what he was doing as we sped along. The headlights revealed what seemed like a single-tracked snow-covered road. We were heading for a ski lodge somewhere in the darkness in front of us, owned and run by an ex-Royal Marine, our home for the next ten days. We were there to learn to ski and survive out in the sub-zero Norwegian winter. The ski lodge turned out to be very comfortable accommodation, built of pine and a very large picture window looked out onto the snow-covered mountains. The lounge had a large blazing fire in its hearth in the evening. Rjukan was famous, or infamous, for its production of heavy water in WWII, which the Germans needed for their efforts to crack the atom. Later for the film 'The Heroes of Telemark'.

We were a party of sixteen, four from the 'C' Squadron under the tender care of two Royal Marines. First being instructed in the art of 'Waxing' our skis, I found, to my surprise, they were not flat but slightly curved up in the middle, needing two waxes one at each end, shone to a gloss and a different type in the middle for grip when the ski is pressed down. The military skis we came to call 'Planks', as they were very robust, wide and, compared to civilian skis, heavy.

Our first outing was going to be on the flat snow out the rear of the lodge. Being the first to finish lunch break and not wanting to look like a fool, I took my skis and walked around the back on the lodge's veranda. Once there, I laid my skis down with the intention of standing on the snow, then went onto my skis. Stepping off, my legs sank up to my thighs and I learned lesson one: the snow was very deep!

To make the administration easier or possibly to appease our Norwegian hosts, we were in civilian clothes, although we had our Bergens and winter wind proofs with us, and in my case, a duck down-filled body warmer made by Georgina's clever hands. Training consisted of putting on your skis, swinging my Bergen onto my back and setting off. At the start, I almost immediately fell over. Then I discovered that you cannot just push yourself up off the snow, because your arm sinks in.

So the routine was to take off your Bergen, sit on it, stand up, swing the Bergen back on for another few metres before a repeat performance. It was exhausting, but slowly we gained distance and confidence between falls as we started tackling the 'Nursery' slopes. Each morning, young Norwegian kids whizzed by on their skis going to school while we, put to shame, struggled along as best we could.

As the days went on, we gained confidence, learning to master more techniques. First, mild down hills, then more undulating ground as well as the exhausting herringbone method of getting uphill. At the end of week one, we had the choice of doing the long gentle winding slope down to the valley floor or the steep 'Black' run. Opting for the latter, I found myself hurtling down through and between the pines, ducking under branches and still shaking for some minutes after blasting out into the bright sunshine at the bottom. Not all made it, one broke his ski on a tree, but fortunately, nothing else. The ski was repaired with the kit the army provided, that was to come very much in handy later on in the course.

Into the second week, we followed several cross-country routes, in and around the surrounding hills. Stopping in one isolated gap in the forest, I found the absolute silence slightly unnerving and was glad to get on my way. We learned how to build snow holes, burrowing into snowdrifts, hollowing and forming a ledge inside if possible, and towards the end of week two, we went out on a two-day route that involved staying out overnight. Late afternoon on the first day, with the light and the temperature dropping, we found what we thought was a large mound of snow discovered, but after several minutes' digging, we discovered it was just a snow-covered rock. The situation started to get serious, as another "snow" mound also proved to be rock.

It was now seriously cold and nearly dark. Someone remembered we had passed a Norwegian hut that the locals used in the summer as a base for hiking and the like. It was a no brainer. We skied back to the hut and found the door locked. We used the hacksaw in our repair kit to gain entry into the small but very welcome interior.

Getting a brew on and some hot food, we spent a pleasantly comfortable, although cramped, night. The next morning, leaving the place clean and tidy, we froze the lock back into place and went on our way to complete the circuit. We made the final RV without revealing our night's accommodation, which we thought the others did not need to know. We hoped when the puzzled Norwegians found their lock sawn off on their next visit, they would realise it would have been because of a serious situation and had forgiveness in their hearts.

On the last days, we had the use of civilian skis. Wearing these was like the difference between wearing boots and trainers. After some practice, I took the Norwegian seven-mile cross-country ski test and passed as a sliver standard cross-country skier.

Monday morning, back to work.

Arrested

On one of our 'working' trips to Germany, we had some excitement when Jim and I were arrested by border guards! Two, with side arms drawn, insisted we went with them! (Komm mit uns!) They escorted us back to their guard base. Some snapping and snarling took place in German at us by the officer in charge. The situation was not helped because at the time, it was our practice to not wear any rank, insignia or berets! We presumed our captors were telling us (what we already knew) that we were in some sort of a prohibited area. We smiled politely and handed over our 'get out of jail card' contact details that we had been given at the briefing by a 'Colonel Flowers' at 1Brit Corp HQ[13] complete with a telephone number. The 'GruppenFuhrer' immediately cranked up his field telephone and made the call. Putting the phone back on its cradle, he indicated that we were good to go. The two guards escorted us back to friendly territory!

As has been mentioned, it was common in the field not to wear any rank insignia. For some reason, we in 'C' Sqn had been issued with US forage caps. This caused problems from time to time. On one occasion, whilst on regimental

---

[13] 1 Brit Corps, 1st British Corps headquarters

duties in Germany, we were going into the nearest army base to POL army jargon for filling up with fuel. We very often took the opportunity to get some 'scoff' in the cookhouse. Standing at the pumps filling the Land Rovers' under-seat tanks, I could see a diminutive RSM[14] was making a beeline for me. Coming up to look me up and down, obviously disapproving of my lightweight windproof smock and US forage cap, he asked, "What army are you in?"

Replying respectively, I said, "British Army, sir." He went on the demand for what unit. I replied our standard, "Corps Patrol Unit[15], sir." I knew the RSM probably had never heard of the Corps Patrol Unit, the non-deplume we used when working in small groups. Not wishing to reveal he didn't know what it was, he grunted, about turned and marched off! Bill, my partner who had come back by that time from a recce to the cookhouse, had a good laugh at the encounter with the camp's non-commissioned supremo. Then, we were off to enjoy our breakfast. The mystery remains today, who is 'Colonel Flowers?' Whoever he was, we still owe him a beer!

Tea, biscuits and broken windows

Not all our activities were in uniform, we role-played on occasions, sometimes helping in the 'fieldcraft' training of the security services and at other times, testing security of various establishments. This time it was RAF Halton's turn!

---

[14] RSM, regimental sergeant major, a very powerful figure

[15] Corp Patrol Unit. Because we "worked" directly for the corps commander, using this title gave us considerable leverage if challenged

Pressing the button to lower the window of my partner Chris's black Granada car, I explained to the guard at the gate that we were expected. Both of us 'Booted and suited' walked into the RAF Hendon's guardroom, asking for the duty officer. I produced my fake police ID card, announcing we had come to check the armoury. We explained to the mystified and slightly alarmed officer that the camp should have had a fax saying we were calling. Of course, he hadn't, so producing my counterfeit fax copy, I explained that we had recently made an arrest and had found a breechblock of a submachine gun (*SMG*) on his property. The arrested man claimed it had come from this very armoury. At that very moment, we were interrupted by Jim coming into the guardroom dressed in a donkey jacket and a flat cap, explaining he had come to mend the broken window in the library. Through the open door, we could see Jim's van complete with a roof rack and ladder parked across the road. The now flustered officer asked him if he knew where it was. Jim indicated that he did, knowing that it was he who had broken the widow with a brick the night before. He was told to carry on (*partial success*). We now had one man unattended inside the camp with a vanload of God knows what! A much older and experienced flight sergeant had, by this time, appeared. He looked concerned but could not intervene as the officer unlocked the armoury door, leading us inside. There we found two rows of SMGs stacked in racks and secured by a chain through their trigger guards. We explained to the officer that we needed them unchained as to compare the number stamped on the breechblock, with the (fictitious) one on our fax. Once the weapons were unchained, laboriously we took out each weapon, checking its number and replacing it back in place.

Finishing off our bogus search, we sat down to tea and biscuits. The officer disappeared and the flight sergeant took over the conversation. It wasn't long before I detected a look of suspicion in his eye, so finishing up our tea, we said we had better be on our way. We exited very shortly after, following Jim's white van out of the gate towards nearby Wendover.

Later in, George and Dragon enjoyed a welcome pint and were grinning at each other, recounting our experience. We were wondering what the station commander was going to say to his boss, who knew the queen was visiting the following week. That three men, possibly armed, had been not only in the camp but also in the armoury! I don't know where the young officer was posted next but probably east of Kathmandu!

The Triangle

The reader might be thinking that my army commitments rolled on one after the other. Well, to an extent that was true, they did. But sometimes with considerable periods in between, before the 'triangle' turned again from family and work to the army. In the early years, only the minimum was required. Later, doing much more was necessary.

The seeds had all been set way back in 1950, when father had moved the family to Leighton Buzzard to take up the position of clerk to the works. Being the youngest, I did all my growing up there, leaving school at fifteen without any qualifications and was destined, like my elder siblings, to earn a living in industry in one dimension or another.

I won my first job against a competing schoolmate, to become a 'Boy' in the maintenance workshop of a roof tile factory. I spent a great deal of time crawling in and around the production line, with the oil can in hand. I moved later when Brother Peter, who had reached the dizzy heights of lance corporal in his national service days, got me a job in an engineering factory. From there, again, I was being lured away to the GPO (*General Post Office),* by the promise of more money and where this story of 'Fought a Million Battles' all started.

In the meantime, I met my one and only love, Georgina, at our local Saturday night 'hop'. The dance had records one week and the 'Barron Knights' the next. Entry cost 'half a dollar' (*25p in today's money*) or a dollar, respectively. Most of my peers like me danced to the popular rock and roll music of the time.

Usually, the girls would all sit on one side of the hall and us boys on the other. So, to ask for a dance you had to risk the 'walk of shame' if you were refused. No one had any formal dance lessons, so some dances went well and others not quite so. Leighton was a small market town and we lads knew most of the local girls. I had seen Georgina about, clicking along in her short skirt and high heels. But she never responded to my calls of "Hello, darling, what are you doing tonight?"

We always thought she was a bit 'stuck up'. Nevertheless, seeing her one Saturday night, I asked her to dance; she accepted and we 'clicked'. We kept dancing together the rest of the night. I was joking later with my mate, Dave Seravenna, that we had tossed a coin to see who had to ask her to dance and I had lost!

She was lovely, beautifully formed with laughing eyes and a ready smile. Walking her home later, she allowed me to kiss her lovely soft lips goodnight. I obviously wanted to see her again! The rest as they say is history; we married in 1965 at just nineteen.

Len Corbett, who you will remember came into my life when I joined the Green Jackets, worked in the flooring trade. Thousands of houses being built is not a new thing, and huge housing conurbations were going up in the 1960s, to accommodate the 'London Overspill' as it was known. There was no shortage of work and at Len's invitation, I joined him to work for Dunlop Semtex, one of the country's major flooring companies. With my Parris family's practical bent, soon picked up the basics, working in the trade for many years. First with Len, then later when he was promoted to the position of a contract manager, I was self-employed.

This formed the triangle, although I did not realise at the time what were to become the three most important things in my life for many years.

Georgina only recently asked why I never joined the regular army. Not having a ready answer, I reasoned that marrying and settling down and the need to earn more money led me to the territorials and cast the die of becoming a volunteer.

North of the Border

Jamie put his hand up. "Yes?" said the boffin from Porton Down. "I've had terrible runs, says Jamie."

"What pill were you on?" he asked.

"Pill A," came the reply.

"That's strange," said the scientists, "that one was a placebo; it was only chalk!"

The room full of soldiers collapsed with laughter bringing the debriefing on our field trials to a close. Ten days earlier as part of the regiment's annual camp in Scotland, we had been given either pill 'A' or 'B', one of which was supposed to give the user protection for a few seconds longer, against nerve agents, to put his respirator on. We had, as part of our daily routine, to keep a record of our bowel movements and other anomalies while out in the field. Clearly Jamie had either had some bad curries or too many prunes.

We had all been through the weekend NBC (*nuclear, chemical and biological*) warfare course at Porton Down, a second time for me, having been through it with the Green Jackets. We all got the CS gas treatment in the gas tent and lived and slept in our 'noddy' suits (*NBC suit*) for twenty-four hours, hoping we would never have to wear them for real.

We weren't north of the border, however, to be guinea pigs for the army to test pills on us, something that probably would not be allowed today. But it was to exercise against some of the multiple military targets in Scotland that might be attacked if the Cold War turned hot.

As I recall, we had a new training major, a regular officer, who was responsible for all our training and was also probably earning his own passage up to staff level; he had injected new enthusiasm into our activities. On one occasion before a night of 'live firing' experience (*using live ammunition*), he said we were all going to be terrified. The exercise turned out to be advancing the wrong way up a knee-high barbed wire infested range. While two machine guns on fixed lines (*mounted on tripods*) were firing streams of tracer bullets towards us ten or fifteen feet or so above our heads, it certainly was a new experience.

Arriving by helicopter to Gairloch head

In Scotland, everything was on a need-to-know basis. It was new for us on a regimental level, so it was not until later we learned what others had been involved in. Some had parachuted into the lock and gained entry into a nuclear submarine, another one of our patrols, training to RV, boarded a submarine at night, using torches with red and green filters on the two boats involved, with a paracord line between them. So the sub could then sail between them, submerged of course. With periscope raised, they were towed them to a point where it was safe to surface. Dave, one of our own, found himself stranded on the casing as the Gemini boat with the rest of his patrol slipped back off the wet hull, disappearing into the darkness. He said later that it was the longest and loneliness he had ever felt until the boat came back for a second round and as it turned out to be a successful attempt.

Our half-troop of eight were tasked with an 'attack' on the RAF Peterhead, a radar station looking out over the North Sea. We did gain access with difficulty, over the ten-foot-high fence. We could have gone through, as a single wire cut in the right place opens up a hole in seconds (*that sort of thing is not allowed on exercise*). But then failed to gain access to an air vent we had seen on the aerial photographs, which led to the underground control centre; it was far too small even for slim Jim's body. But any sort of charge dropped down would not have been welcome for real. Also, easy pickings for a surprise visit were the huge and vulnerable revolving radar scanner. Hopefully, all these lessons the RAF learned that night resulted in a re-think of their defences. Once the 'balloon' went up *(the alarm being sounded)*, it was time to go. The memory of Frank struggling to get over the fence going in and nearly vaulting it going out has stayed with me ever since. As did our night departure from Gairloch head.

The helipad was in a clearing above the camp in a wooded area accessed via a dirt track. After dark, the three-tonner transport took us up to meet the incoming helicopter. It growled its way up in low gear, headlights illuminating the trees either side until entering into the helipad's clearing.

As we swung round, they fell on a car with steamed up windows. For what seemed an eternity, nothing happened. Then a bare arse appeared against the back window as someone tried to get over it into the front without his trousers. Seconds later, the three-tonner started up and was roaring off down the track to our assembled jeers and laughter.

These memories are all merging into one after all these years. I think our return journey back to our nearest airfield to Hitchin, RAF Henlow, was by aircraft and a daylight jump. Regardless if it was then or another occasion. Our families, forewarned, were there to meet us, and it was a very welcome homecoming. Monday morning, of course, was back to work!

Let's Get the Hell Out of Here

We had left the Land Rover some fifty yards back and started walking along the track in the dark, hopelessly looking for signs that the poachers, who had shot a small herd of elephants earlier in the day, might have crossed on their way back to the Somali border.

Moving off into the bush in the direction they must have taken, my heart stopped for a second, hearing the deep growl of lions. Knowing they were about – it was after all a game reserve but we had not realised that the pride had moved into our area – was pretty scary. In the darkness, it was near impossible to either see or smell them. The lions, on the other hand, are quite able to do both. It was time to go; I slipped the safety off on my weapon and knelt down, back against a thorn bush. I whispered to the regular who was out with me, "I have got an idea."

"What's that?" came the whispered reply. Looking up against the night sky to hopefully silhouette anything approaching us, I said, "Let's get the hell out of here!" We did.

It was the mid-1970s, and four of us had travelled to Kenya as part of a small team of 21, to train the soldiers from the Royal Corps of Signals. Over a four-week period, they would be alternating between us in the Samburu Game Park and the team from 22 on the side of Mount Kenya. We were to train them in 'combat survival' (*survival navigation, traps and trapping*) along with living and navigating in the jungle. The objective was both giving the signallers part practical and part adventure training. We had flown down to the capitol on an ancient Britannia with the first batch of signal guys.

After a night stop in RAF Akrotiri in Cyprus and an evening meal in the mess, complete with white-coated waiters, we set off after dark, again flying south down the Nile Delta towards our destination. Once over the delta, the captain announced to say that a light aircraft had gone off the radar and we had been requested to investigate.

The lights were dimmed as we descended. Because we, on the training team, had binoculars with us and were asked to make our way back to look out of the door portholes to help spot the downed aircraft in the darkness. It was not long after the plane had descended – positioning myself in the door and looking out into the night sky as the 'Brit' circled – we saw a light flashing orange in the darkness. Turning to attract the steward's attention, he was fortunately walking away, I looked again realising that the flashing light wasn't from the ground but a reflection of the fuselage strobe light on the underside of the hidden wingtip in the darkness. I swiftly put my arm down. Just then a long way down in the blackness, a vairy flair made its tiny lazy parabolic arc in the desert. We had found them. After making contact, our pilot told us that the people on the ground were fine but had a minor problem which was safely fixed and the we droned on our way south in the morning.

Once 'in country', we had about a week to wait for the first group to come through, so we joined the 22 guys up on the side of Mount Kenya. The first thing that surprised me was how bitterly cold up on the mountain it was first thing in the morning, with a white frost on everything not under the canopy of the jungle. Our senior rank, Alan, was a sergeant and I, by then, was a corporal, the other two being troopers. We all came under the command of their senior rank, a warrant officer class one (WO1). We were almost immediately put to work, two of us being tasked to do a 'recce' (*reconnaissance*) for a two-day route up and around the mountain for the pupils to follow under their own NCOs. To my dismay, when I asked Dave, the WO1, for ammunition, I was told that none had arrived. It was not a comforting thought to spend two days and a night in thick bush, full of elephants, water buffalos and gorillas (*although they may have recognised us as a similar tribe*), with nothing more than our shirts in front of us. After discussing the route, we set off on the climb out. The days walking proved to be uneventful. As the light began to fail, we backed ourselves into a very thick thorn bush, blocking the entrance with our Bergens. I'm not sure what Alan did in the darkness but for me, I lay awake most of the night, with my knife drawn, listening to 'things' padding past us in the darkness. During the few days, we were temporarily made homeless, as after a huge and sudden downpour of rain, a colony of wood ants was washed out (*each about ½" long*). They came through our basha site, first in a trickle that grew to a yard wide torrent. We had no choice but to stand aside and watch until the colony finally passed, presumably to a dryer spot.

A few days later, we set off for the long ride north to the Samburu Game Park in the north of the country. We stopped for the night at the little town of Nanuki, situated at the end of the tarmac road. From there, nothing was present for hundreds of miles except tracks up to the Somali border. We were having a quiet beer in the ramshackle B&B when the night security came by, and a very large local gentleman, carrying an equally large lump of wood, walked through the bar. He also wore an old British army great coat complete with a toy policeman's helmet, his symbol of power on his head. We all buried our noses in our beers while he stalked past. After another day driving on terrible tracks, we found ourselves in the Samburu. There we found the advanced party commanded by a Royal Marine, who had named the camp Rorke's Drift, complete with a small staff of regulars in support. Over the next four weeks, we got on with training batches of the young signallers. We were charged with teaching survival navigation, which is quite tricky on the equator and animal traps. We had to organise trapping live rabbits for the students as food for the day. There were quite a few white faces in the ranks when demonstrating first how to kill quickly, skin and gut. After three days, the signallers had a two-day final exercise before departure to the camp on Mount Kenya. Once one group had departed and before the next arrived, we had a twenty-four-hour break in the luxury of the Samburu Lodge, some twenty miles away.

The lodge, very upmarket, was served by a light aircraft to bring in its VIP guests. We had the luxury of a shower, great food served to our table and a cool beer in hand. We could watch a leopard come for its evening meal, feasting on a carcass strung up in a floodlight tree the other side of the river. We ended the night in a soft bed.

On one rest period, we gave up all of this because we had heard that Concorde 002 was in Nairobi where the runway, at 12,000 foot high, was ideal for high altitude engine tests. We could not miss this opportunity so four of us drove all day and through the night to get to the airport. Arriving there about nine in the morning, we found the aircraft surrounded by Kenyan armed guards. Being in uniform ourselves, we brazenly walked out across the tarmac, feeling very exposed, straight past the guards, whom we ignored, and went up to the aircraft. Underneath, we found the chief test pilot John Cunningham and some technicians in discussion. When he saw us coming, he just said, "Morning, have a look around lads, just don't touch anything."

All the final exercises were notional E&E ones across the area, with a few of the base guys as the hunter force. On one of the occasions, we had a garbled radio message to say someone was down with heat stroke, but they could not give us their position. We split into two groups, climbed two nearby hills and then radioed the patrol to fire a flair. This allowed both our groups to take bearings and triangulate where the casualty was. All four of us then set off on what was to be a twelve-hour cross-country night drive through thick bush, up and down ravines and over rocks and boulders. We reached the group the next morning, to find they had no water left but on inspection we found they still had loads of foot powder. Cooled down with water and rested, the casualty soon recovered and we brought him back to base. Arriving there, we saw that all the green paint had been stripped off the front end of the rover.

On another occasion, while going down to the river to see a returning signals patrol with the OC, we saw, to our alarm, a crocodile under the bank; a round of 7.62 seemed to sort the problem, allowing the group to cross safely and in record time. Sadly, a few weeks later, we came across a small herd of elephants that had been machine-gunned by Somali poachers and the ivory taken. We offered to help the hopelessly small and poorly armed band of rangers to track these people down, having done a tracking course down in New Zealand (*Georgina would never have believed that I was a trained tracker as now I cannot even find my own socks*). This led us to the night's excitement with lions and of our five weeks away.

We did hear later that the Kenyans had got themselves a poacher. For us, back to Blighty and work the following Monday.

Kenyan termite mound.

WOII

By 1979, I had reached the dizzy heights of warrant officer class two (WOII); at the time, I was very proud and honoured to be promoted, becoming one of the youngest WOII in the regiment and quite possibly the SAS group.

Looking back at the squadron, it must have been desperate to choose me from amongst so many of my capable peers, but they had and with my promotion came the position of squadron sergeant major. Over the next two years, I became very involved in the organisation of any squadron activities. I was responsible for discipline and working with and reporting directly to my 'Boss', Bill.

That year, we went to America; this was my first visit. We were a mixed troop from 'C' and the other 'out' (*outside London*) squadron 'D' in Portsmouth. We joined the 11th Specials Forces in the huge Pennsylvania forests, handling US weapons and equipment. We were tasked to patrol with our US colleagues against our 'enemy', some US Navy guys. Some of the Americans seemed very fit and capable, while others left us slightly puzzled and we were asking ourselves, "Are these really 'special forces'?" On one occasion, we were being shown how to strip down and reassemble an M60 machine gun. The demonstrator tried and failed to put the working parts back in upside down until Dave took over, showing the embarrassed American the correct way.

Dave shows how it's done Brit army meets navy SEAL

There were plenty of opportunities to parachute using the American T10. It was larger than ours and the Americans jumped from 1,200 ft as opposed to our 800 for training and as low as 400, if required. We had a competition to see who could land closest to a marker on the DZ. We all failed miserably, none of us landed closer than fifty odd yards, with the unfamiliar equipment.

Jumping from a helicopter four each side, feet on the skids, the 'Boss' was first, I was second and then the remaining two on our side of the aircraft. While approaching the DZ, the noise and wind inside the aircraft made Bill think that the shouting and arm waving from the jumpmaster meant go! He immediately disappeared from view and I nearly followed him when the cry of anguish stopped me, realising that the gesticulating and shouting was not the signal to jump. Circling around, we could see that Bill was floating down towards a lone tree. If he tried to steer away or not, we never knew, but land in the tree he did.

We all jumped a few minutes later and found Bill having an argument with a medic who had arrived in an ambulance, demanding that he lay down on a stretcher to be taken away and be examined for injuries. He did not have the patience. In the end, it condescended to "at least get in the ambulance for a check over and ride back", all to our amusement.

'Lema' Troop

We left a few days later, flying from Pease Air Force base in Maine. The Hercules climbed its way out; we settled down for a long and noisy flight across the Atlantic. Shortly after levelling off, smoke started to drift into the fuselage; this caused quite a bit of alarm, as we had no parachutes and even if we did, we were by them quite away from the coast.

The crewman started urgently clambering about shining his torch into the dark recesses inside the aircraft. We rapidly started losing height and were being told that some of the lagging around trunking that bled heat from an inboard engine had caught fire. Presumably, the heating was shut down and shortly after, we found ourselves alighting in Gander Newfoundland.

For the next few days, we amused ourselves by going for runs along the pine-lined roads and playing cards in the evening until a spare arrived three days later, only then continuing what was an uneventful flight home. It brought an end to my penultimate foray to foreign fields. Next Monday, back to work.

My second visit to America came a year later. Between the two visits, a group from 11SFG had been with us in Scotland. Their lieutenant, after a late arrival at an RV, told me he had never experienced sun, rain and snow all in one day. He said, "My boys are fit and tough, we just didn't expect this." We were back again in the US with the 11th Special Forces Group in Pennsylvania, where the local police chief in a briefing warned us about going down into the 'combat zone' in nearby Boston.

This was reinforced when two of the guys invited me to go into town for a beer. I agreed first, but later seeing them putting their 9mm automatics in shoulder holsters, I decided that perhaps it wasn't such a good idea after all.

The Americans, as hospitable as ever, arranged for us to fire their weapons, an amazing range from all over the world. Some types we had never seen before. We spent time on the ranges, using what they call C4 *(Plastic explosive)* and their communication equipment, which we found light years behind ours. There were lectures in the hot airless lecture room, where we endured some awfully presented lectures. Many found it almost impossible to keep awake, myself included, perfecting the art of resting my chin in my hand, pencil in the other, notebook open and resting my eyes.

We had each evening off. Two of us went, by mistake, into a 'black' bar. We could almost feel the hostility until we ordered a beer. Confirming the barman's question of "are you guys from England?", the hostility for the most part dissipated; nevertheless, we didn't overstay our welcome!

The base bar had permanently low lighting, so regardless of what time you went in, it always seemed late evening and leaving after a beer or two and emerging into bright sunshine was always startling. One night, there was a 'wet t-shirt' competition. It was all fixed, of course, on appeal for lady volunteers from the crowd. A lovely young woman immediately stepped up onto the stage amid cheers and laughter. With encouragement from the crowd, others soon followed until five or six had joined her. We were in the front row and decided we would vote for the most buxom lady. After each pouring of beer, the one with least cheers was eliminated until two were left, our buxom favourite and unlikely winner and the lovely stooge. We were cheering our loudest for our choice. The compere pretended not to see or hear us, looked out over the assembled audience and declared the stooge as the winner.

The final two-day exercise involved some training on the technique of 'Hot extraction' *(lifted out from very dangerous or difficult situations),* where the helicopter came with line and harnesses lowered. The troops were on the ground, four being the maximum, putting on the harness as the chopper lifted up and away as soon as possible. It was a slightly hairy experience, swinging about on the end of a rope, hoping you had clicked all the buckles in place.

The jump in that night from a C128, a sort of twin-engine Hercules, landing in some sort of boggy grassy DZ, got down low so as to silhouette my half troop *(eight men)* in the darkness to see where they were, only to see clouds of mosquitoes around each one. Knowing that they must be the same around me and my sweat-soaked jungle fatigue top, which would be like a magnet. We also had two rather disgruntled 22 blokes attached to us. They didn't seem very happy having to be under the command or with a TA unit, making them independent lead scouts and later rear guards, as we withdrew from the target attack, VIP snatch exercise, resolved their problem. The 'attack' was the first major one within my sole responsibility, inheriting it by virtue of my being the senior rank.

The plan and dry training run through in the day, all going wrong in a night full of dazzling trip flares, muzzle flashes and exploding thunder flashes. I learned the lesson that one of the first casualties of a contact is always the plan.

We never used 'hot extraction', but once back in camp, with my shirt off, I could see dozens of bites across my back and arms. The American medic came around. When I showed him my bites, he assured me they had just the stuff. Expecting some magical solution to my discomfort, I was disappointed when he produced a large bottle of calamine lotion!

We were due to fly back by RAF VC10 but on arrival in Washington, we found our seats had been taken by some VIPs who had priority. We were told to wait until further orders. Making use of the next three days hanging about, I was able to see the White House and visit the spectacular Smithsonian Museum. New orders never arrived. Talking to our colonel back in England, we decided the only thing we could do was to catch a civilian flight. Some standby seats came up and shortly after, we flew home in two groups, finally arriving back in the UK a week later than expected. Our colonel later, very sportingly, reimbursed us from his own purse. Monday morning, again back to work.

A Little or a Lot

A TA soldier could just do just the minimum required or get involved full time and some did. We were all paid on the pro rata scales and a once-a-year bonus. In the early days, £100 was quite sufficient for me to buy a 'new' second-hand car. Most volunteers who had completed selection, continuation and para course, however, were very committed. I found this increasing as my rank and responsibilities grew over the years.

Weekend training might include tactical landing strips, starting with a lecture. It then would continue under RAF supervision, using the RAF's local training field. It included laying out of a flare path 1,200 by 150 ft for the Hercules to land on. You would have to wait after dark, torch in hand, for the aircraft to appear out of the darkness, its wingtip almost sweeping over your head as it landed on the grass strip. Then, you would start running like hell as it turned, to run up its ramp into the dim red lit inside of the fuselage, before taking off back to RAF Lynham.

*Mortar training   Winner 'Falling plate'**

On other weekends, we were introduced to the basics of explosives. The exercise was conducted with both the standard NATO charge or improvised devices, using such things as a wine bottle, to make a hollow charge that could incredibly send its concave bottom into a molten slug that penetrated the armour of an old conqueror tank. Ring mains using a 'det' cord that burned at 24,000 ft per second. Time pencils the colours remembered by the acronym to this day: 'British rail will get you back'*. Pull, pressure and release switches and so on. At the end of the weekend, I almost got stuck on the short test, as my maths let me down.

The answer to the question of 'what is the quantity of plastic explosives needed to cut through steel' is arrived at by using a formula. Knowing the fraction-based formula but not having a grasp on fractions, my answer, 'P for Plenty', got me a pass.

Adventure and fitness training in North Wales were often the subject of a lot of weekend training. These would consist of another late night arrival, this time in Llanberis, where we had the use of a room in the back of the local pub. A full day's walk the next day always included the peak of Snowden. We ending with riotous nights by climbing out of the back window. After hours, we would be back in our quarters. Sunday morning was always a fast ascent up the Snowden light railway track and back; it cleared away any headache before returning back to Hitchin and home. We would usually stop for an all-day breakfast on the way.

Small groups of the regiment very often took part in much longer one-off exercises. These were in addition to the annual 'camp' and very often as part of a much larger NATO exercise. We also took part in exchange visits with foreign armies and on occasions joined our regular regiment. Specialist teams at home and abroad were dispatched to teach skills that any particular units needed. Role-playing for people from the security services as part of their 'field craft' training.

From time to time, I became involved in operational matters that come under the 'need to know rules' and are not covered in these pages.

Those of us who were married had a balanced family and army work year in and year out. Not all partnerships survived though.

What a Pigsty!

Slowly crawling my way to the edge of the wood, I looked down on the small German hamlet below me. At first, all looked quiet. Scanning with my binoculars, I saw a man standing at the corner of one of the outbuildings, having a smoke. Almost at the same time, I realised he was standing under the edge of a large camouflage net that stretched up to the building's eave. Looking behind him, I saw more nets, a lot more. In fact, most of the buildings were camouflaged to some degree. We had found it! An 'enemy' divisional HQ.

That night, we went in close to have a look around, careful not to alarm any sentries and to confirm what we had found. Getting straight on, the 'net' (*radio*) reported the location. At first light, two Harrier jets shattered the morning quiet, one after the other blasting over our heads and the hamlet in a simulated air strike, putting division headquarters out of the exercise.

Last light squadron briefing

Acting as 'orange' *(exercise enemy)* forces had given us quite a lot of freedom, our brief to seek out 'blue' (*NATO*) headquarters, nuclear delivery systems and other assets for air strikes. The division HQ was a definite feather in our caps.

Two nights previously, I was standing at the edge of a wood alongside a track that led to a field workshop we had found. Two German officers came out in their jeep and stopped right alongside me to confer. I was standing, watching with interest as they talked.

Then without warning, an M113 *(a large tracked armoured personnel carrier)* came up behind them and without stopping, it crashed through the wood where we were standing. We reeled backwards very nearly finishing up under its tracks as it slewed onto the road and sped off at full throttle. A very close shave.

We had also spent several days living with a load of pigs in an outbuilding of a farm, road watching and reporting back on vehicle numbers and types from the loft above.

The pigs, all in large square pens, would stand up with front legs over their gates as we passed to and fro on the ground floor. At night, in torch light, it was like Dante's Inferno walking between them, instinctively keeping your arms by your side. The stench was awful and on occasions, I could not help retching. We couldn't go out in the daylight but opened one of the large doors a fraction to sit and breathe clean air. It brought a smelly end to my last time with the squadron in the field.

EndEx (end of exercise) and last annual camp with the squadron.

Completing the Circle

With my compulsory two years coming to an end as sergeant major, new horizons and pathways started to appear. It seemed light years before when the new boss by then, Frank, had been one of those sat on their Bergens at the Taff Trail RV, where I had also failed on my first selection.

The process of the next senior NCO to be promoted and take over was well underway. For me, a position at 'group' was offered; that would mean transferring from squadron to our HQ in London. This was heading up to a new cell looking at options for 'offensive ops' (*offensive operations)* against, at the time, our major adversaries, the Warsaw pact armies.

The idea looked very interesting but leaving the squadron and travelling to London on a regular basis was not. As there is only the entitlement for one WOII per squadron; the alternative was to stay with the squadron and to run our end of the selection process but at the reduced rank of sergeant.

The move to selection was probably for the best because of the previous year's deployment to Germany. We had gone into the field with ten days of all the paraphernalia that a patrol needs to operate, which resulted in each of us having massively overloaded Bergens. After the drop off, the weight of our bergens forced us take turns to sit on the floor, put on the shoulder straps and then be hauled up by two other members onto our feet.

Towards the end of the exercise on the exfiltration out that night, we had to cross a small river. Looking at the map, there was a tiny mark on it that signified a footbridge. We were weighing the risk of using the bridge or going through the process of making a proper river crossing. I slipped out of my Bergen and went forward in order to have a look. Satisfied that the tiny bridge was completely deserted, I returned to the waiting patrol. Then instead of going through the usual routine to stand up with two mates helping me, I simply swung the Bergen up on my back. Almost immediately, I felt an intense pain in my spine. I realised I had injured myself, but at the same time, I had the responsibility of leading my patrol back to friendly territory and we carried on. The pain in my back did not seem too bad, being well warmed up after the long walk to the river crossing. But once cooled down and when I sat still for some time, it became extremely uncomfortable. Getting back to base after the pickup and going to see our MO should have my first priority but for some reason, I never gave it a thought and struggled on sorting things out, ready to travel back.

Arriving home, the injury was far too painful to work, and being self-employed meant no work no pay. So urgently, I saw an orthopaedic surgeon privately. After an x-ray, the surgeon confirmed he could see a slipped disc. The solutions offered were either to wear a corset or have two vertebrae fused together. Neither of these filled me with enthusiasm.

Over that weekend, my squash partner called to ask why our scheduled game was off. After I told him the reason, he advised me to see a Mr Triance, our local osteopath. I gave him a call and explained the situation; he opened up his surgery for me the next day. He massaged and manipulated my back and with a final twist and clonk that made me grunt, he put my spine back together. I was told to take it easy for a few days and was soon back at work*. But the risk of further injury made the decision to join the training wing the right one at the end of my tenure.

I am somewhere in this group

21 SAS Selection Course Summer 1981
273 . . . the biggest ever. 11 passed. The moment of truth as 273 form-up for briefing from the PSI Chief Instructor of Training Wing. What is not shown is the suicide of the QM and his storeman after the efforts involved in clothing and equipping a group which was three times the size of the average course.

So, in 1981, I joined the 'Wing' to take on the ten 'C' squadron recruits who had signed up for the next selection. The whole regiment had a massive 273 recruits, the biggest ever that year as a result of the publicity surrounding the raid on the Iranian Embassy. This huge number had already been whittled down from an even larger number in interviews and medicals. Only eleven were to pass, two from 'C' Sqn.

The huge number that started our biggest ever selection course ever meant that we, the staff, had to start with quite large numbers to look after.

All the selection courses had a WO1 in command, as well as several other regulars. During that time, it was my privilege to work with some very notable characters from 22, several losing their lives later in the terrible night of the helicopter incident in the Falklands War.

By the time of our first visits to the Brecons and the first conducted walk, my party was down to a dozen or so. Having crossed the stream on the series of rocks that had now been placed as stepping-stones, where I had the 'Welsh wax' experience many years earlier, I directed them on up the 'Fan'. Bringing up the rear group, I saw very shortly after that one was already limping and did not look like he was going to get to the end of today's 'tour'. Overtaking them, I pressed onto the memorial of little Tommy Jones*. I stopped and the group started to come by. Our lame recruit was now limping on the other leg. As he came up to me, I enquired why the change of the leg. He told me he couldn't limp on one leg all the while! Needless to say, he failed.

It was always very important to keep an eye on how your group was doing or how someone looked when he came into an RV you were manning. All three of the regiments have had fatalities over the years. The last two were from heat stroke. There a regular officer who had come back to take over a squadron; he had sat down in the area we all called the 'moon country', near the Roman road track junction in the Brecons. He had sat down to rest at night, fell asleep and never woke up, dying of hypothermia.

My personal experience and a brush with hypothermia was on a particular bleak fitness weekend in North Wales. All of us were very wet with a bitterly cold wind cutting across the 'pig track' we were climbing. Joe, the regular PSI to our 63 signals (SASV) squadron, started talking about toy train sets. Realising he was starting to suffer hypothermia, I stopped and got out of the wind, helped him into dry clothes and a sleeping bag. The added threat in these situations is that we were all probably near the danger line. After a short break and a brew that we all enjoyed in the lee of the ridge and a change of some wet to dry clothes with Joe's rapid recovery, we carried on to complete the planned walk.

On occasion, selection was taken in different parts of the country, one in my time was in the North Yorkshire moors. Although not the Brecons, the moors can be just as bleak and unforgiving as the mountains of Wales. There was another fatality when a recruit went missing. Later, his Bergen turned up downstream in the 'Beck', but his body was never found. Although not privy to the full story, it can be assumed the police became involved and followed up with his family. At the time, it was thought he had got into difficulty when crossing the stream, lost his balance and Bergen, perhaps knocking himself unconscious.

By the time the third selection course was coming to an end, I started to feel I had read the book, seen the film and got the t-shirt, and looking ahead, I could not see myself becoming, as some were, a permanent selection jockey. I decided to have a look around to see what else was about.

A Spanner in the Works

That something turned out to be 118 Recovery Company Royal Electrical and Mechanical Engineers. (REME). I vaguely knew them through a mutual friend in the Royal Anglians, who also used the drill hall in Clare St Northampton. I called them with a view of doing something completely different and was immediately offered the position of company sergeant major with promotion immediately back to WOII. How could an offer like that be turned down? So in due course, I transferred from SAS(V) to REME (V) a few weeks later. The Northampton company was one of two, the other being based in Corby, both part of a much bigger support battalion. REME history goes back to the Second World War. By 1942, the need for specialist units was becoming urgent to take pressure off the need for replacements wherever possible.

The modern TA unit has very large eight-wheeled crane-equipped vehicles.

Life in the REME was totally different to that in my former home. Gone were the casual first names used in the squadron; there were, of course, exceptions, such as the OC who are usually called 'Boss' except on formal occasions. In the 118, it was always either sir from below sergeant or sergeant major from an officer. There were other peculiarities in that there were two WOIIs, myself responsible for discipline and making sure that all the background support was in place.

The other WOII was an artificer, a senior mechanic responsible for the vehicles, crews, technical training and the like.

One of 118's main roles in a war-fighting scenario would be to keep the main supply routes (MSRs) open, clearing wrecked vehicles, repairing in situ if possible or recovery if more work was required. Each recovery truck had a four-man crew. This gave me some scope to inject some other interests into the company's drill nights and weekends. In the fluid situation that would occur near the

FEBA (The forward edge of the battle area), they might easily find them cut off without their vehicle.

The introduction of evasion and survival navigation skills were all greeted with enthusiasm.

I incorporated competitive weapon training in teams and not too heavy-handed parades and drill. (*Something I had not had much practice at myself!*) Everything went down well. The guys were basically mechanics but really seemed to enjoy the new angle to their REME soldering.

But making no pretence that I knew anything about recovery or fixing lorries, not to tread on anyone's toes, I made sure we rubbed along okay. Over time, I came to know both the regular captain and staff sergeants well, both of whom seemed very happy with the new broom that had swept through the company.

A photograph from my scrapbook

That year, the company went to Folkestone for its annual camp. The training, much of it already decided before my time and bizarrely, did not include their vehicles.

Apart from my duties, there was very little to do, so I was very much my own boss. Once morning muster parade was over and the guys dispersed to their duties, very often I would go out for a run or join in their training, without interfering but passing on any tips that might be helpful and carrying the company's heaviest weapon on the march and shoots.

The company's sergeants' mess enjoyed its formal functions, dress code being enforced, something that was not my scene but I was expected to attend. My position was quite an isolated one. The essential camaraderie, all part of what had been the norm, was missing and clearly in my mind, my time in the TA was drawing to a close. The Falklands War had, by this time, been fought and won. I was still self-employed in the flooring industry, subcontracting to a Bedford company, who had won a contract to install flooring at the new airfield accommodation on the island's RAF Mount Pleasant. I was asked to join the five-man flooring team for the six-month contract. I took a leave of absence from 118, kissed Georgina goodbye and in early spring 1983, left for the ten-thousand-mile trip via South Africa to the Falklands.

Whilst there, our flooring work rapidly caught up with the construction of the accommodation being erected on the site. As a result, we had a fair amount of free time. So often, I would go out with my camera and on weekends, I would go further out into the 'Campo'. Having a mine threat map borrowed from an army connection on the island, I was able to move about with quite a high degree of safety. I explored Mount Pleasant itself and later teamed up with another 'Territorial' to go as far north as Top Mallow, near the northern coast. Meanwhile, I kept in touch with Georgina through phone calls and later micro tapes, which were sent via the military postal service to our local radio station. They not only broadcast them but sent me blank ones back for more! The six months dragged on and I finally arrived home that summer.

Mount Pleasant Falklands 1992

Returning to 118, any spark that was left had, by that time, gone. I resigned in 1984, having served as a territorial fifteen years and 147 days.

As for the veterans of 'C' Squadron, there is still great camaraderie, as in any close-knit group, with social spin-offs that survive to this day. A walking group started in 1995 after Bill and I bumped into each other many years after leaving the TA. We had coffee and catching up, we found we both still walked. Bill with another group and myself as a footpath's guide for the county.

From these small beginnings, we gathered through the contacts of our old quartermaster sergeant, Colin and squadron members from our 'era'. We started to meet once a month to walk routes all over our part of the country.

At the turn of the century, a new 196-mile coast-to-coast route was established, known as 'The Hobblers Way' (*registered on the Long-Distance Footpath Site).*

Social get-togethers and families' days as well as the annual reunion for all the SAS regiments in the Brecons.

The Hobblers The 'TA100'

Remembrance Sunday 2020

Records and documentation.

Having received the records of my service, I have compiled a list of dates and a small sample of some of the records forwarded to me. They have taken some deciphering as the date of being updated was not, in some cases, some time after the event or do not correspond with other entries.

1st selection dates as 02/03/68 (failed)

Joining the Green Jackets	07/05/69
First promotion to L/cpl	01/08/70
Second promotion to Cpl	24/08/71
Second selection	24/09/71 (passed with loss of rank)
Promotion back to L/cpl	01/04/72

Promotion to Cpl	04/03/74
Promotion to Sgt	08/12/75
Promotion to WOII	01/12/79
Voluntary revert to Sgt	8/12/80
Transfer to 118 Rec Coy	30/06/83 with the rank of WOII
Resigned	24/10/84

Promotions

Some deployments

PART III   (To be completed by applicant's Commanding Officer)

Remarks and recommendations (including character) *Cpl. Hattis is a very good soldier indeed and an outstanding volunteer NCO. He has done very well with us, and we shall be very sorry to lose him.*

Date 17/11/71   Signature of Commanding Officer *J. M. Tisdall Capt.*

PART IV

To:— Officer in Charge Records administering new unit.

INFANTRY RECORDS, HIGHER BKS, EXETER.

No objection to the proposed *posting/transfer
          Commanding

Date 26·11·71   Signature of Officer in Charge
          Records administering present unit. *WKRobertson.*

PART V

     OIC Records Administering New Unit
To:— *Officer Commanding new Unit.*

     Infantry Records Higher Barracks Exeter

     No objection to the proposed *posting/transfer

8 DEC 1971   Signature of Officer in Charge   for Lt Col
Date   Records administering new unit Commanding 21 SAS Regt (Artists) TA

PART VI

Report on leaving 4 RGJ(V)

To:— Officer I/c Records (soldiers' present Regt./Corps)

No objection. Please inform the soldier's present CO and arrange *posting/transfer.

          Officer in Charge
Date 10 DEC 1971 Signature of Officer Commanding new unit

Ref: ASVU/NV/..b.45.   MINISTRY OF DEFENCE
Army Security Vetting Unit
Royal Military Academy
Woolwich, London SE18

Army Network: Woolwich Garrison Military) Ext.
GPO: 01-854-2424   } 354

17 September 1971

...Infantry Record Office...
......Exeter.......

....

INFANTRY RECORD OFFICE
EXETER
22 SEP 1971

NORMAL VETTING NO..........

Reference your ....1|54|184(5)................

dated ...2|8|71......

1.   There is NO SECURITY OBJECTION to ......)....name(s)
mentioned.

2.   The necessary form(s) are attached.

3.   REMARKS

····_Security vetted_····················

....

....

....

Commander
Army Security Vetting Unit

NV/P

972/2 0514 (1) 3/71

PARACHUTING CERTIFICATE

In accordance with Regulations for The T & AVR 1967

I understand that, once having qualified as a
parachutist and whilst serving in an Airborne Unit on
a current parachute tour, I can be ordered to make a
parachute descent at any time of the night or day as
part of my Annual Training, subject to medical fitness
at the time.

On re-engagement, I wish to extend my parachute
tour to the end of my new engagement.

Signed _[signature]_

Number 24139577 Rank TPR Name HARRIS F. W.

(BLOCK LETTERS PLEASE)

Date 20.1.72.

1/72 100

21st SAS Regt (Artists)(V)

REVERSION CERTIFICATE

I, No 24139577 Rank WO2 Name HARRIS FW

wish to apply to revert to the substantive Rank of Sgt

with effect 30 Nov 80

It is certified that this reversion is not to avoid any disciplinary
action

Date 18.12.80 Signature _[signature]_

Conformation of revert to Sgt

PART III

(To be completed by applicant's present Commanding Officer)

Remarks and recommendations (including character) ..... During his 12 years with this regiment, Sgt Harris has displayed many good qualities, particularly as a weapon instructor. He finds difficulty in inspiring a sense of discipline. Although his enthusiasm can be variable, if motivated, can produce excellent results.

Date 10/5/13   Signature of Commanding Officer

PART IV

To:- Officer Commanding new Unit,

        118 Recovery   Coy REME(V)

            No objections to the proposed *posting/transfer.

28 MAY 1983

            Signature of Officer Commanding
Date   present unit.
                                    Lt Col
                        Commanding 21 SASR (Artists) (V)

PART V

To:- Officer in Charge Records administering new unit.

            No objection to the proposed *posting/transfer

            Signature of Officer Commanding
Date   new unit.

PART VI

Less than happy with this report on leaving 21 sas(V)

To:- Officer I/c Records (soldier's present Regt./Corps)

        No objection.   Please inform the soldier's present CO and arrange *posting/transfer.

            Signature of Officer in Charge of Records
Date   administering new unit.

B 200 (ADP)   SOLDIERS RECORD OF SERVICE

                                      DETAIL

52A PRIOR SERVICE FROM   TO   TYPE OF SE(
                020368   100668   T|

56 COURSES ATTENDED   COURSE
                SAS SELECTION   2:
                SAS SELECTION   0

61 MEDALS AND AWARDS (GALLANTRY,FOREIGN & LONG SERVICE)
                          EFFICIENCY MEDAL (TAVR)

5A MOBILISATION DETAILS

    ARC CODE   MOB AREA   REPORTED DATE   UNISSUED KIT SI
    *00000   *,*,*,*,*4*

    CURRENT TAX CODE: 080

    BANK ACCOUNT: TITLE - HARRIS FW&GJ   NUMBER - 0

66 DETAILS OF ANNUAL CAMP / TRG PERIODS

        TRAINING YEAR   CAMP   COURSE   ATTA
                1984   15   0
                1983   24   0
                1982   16   0
                1981   41   0
                1980   45   0
                1979   27   0
                1978   15   0
                1977   15   0
                1976   15   0
                1975   0   14
                1974   15   0

Medals and awards

70 TA UNIT   GROUP A (INDEPENDENT)

71 BASIC TRAINING COMPLETED 060874

71A DATE FIT FOR ROLE 010883

72 NOT QUALIFIED FOR PROMOTION

74 NO RESERVE LIABILITY

TERRITORIAL ARMY

CERTIFICATE OF DISCHARGE

THIS IS TO CERTIFY THAT THE SOLDIER NAMED WAS DISCHARGED
FROM THE TERRITORIAL ARMY ON THE DUE DATE

G Piko

OIC   REME MANNING AND RECORD OFFICE

WARNING

Should this Certificate be lost or mislaid no duplicate will
be issued. In exceptional circumstances a Certificate, on
Army Form B 108A, may be obtained on application to the
Officer in Charge of Manning and Records concerned.

The person to whom this Certificate is issued should on no
account part with it or forward it by post when applying for
a situation but should use a copy.

Any alterations of the particulars given on this Certificate
may render the holder liable to prosecution.

Soldiers leaving Her Majestys Service are reminded that the
unauthorised communication by them to another person AT ANY TIME
of any information they may have acquired which might be useful
to any enemy in war renders them liable to prosecution under the
OFFICIAL SECRETS ACTS.

ANY PERSON FINDING THIS Certificate is requested to forward it

in an unstamped envelope to:-

THE MINISTRY OF DEFENCE (M3(A))

LONDON SW1A 2HB

ARMY FORM B108D(ADP

CERTIFICATE OF SERVICE

NAME	RANK	NUMBER
FW HARRIS	WARRANT OFFICER CL 2	24139577

REGT/CORPS	DATE OF BIRTH
REME	01 AUG 45

UNIT TITLE
115 REC COY

DATE OF ENLISTMENT	REGT/CORPS ON ENLISTMEN
07 MAY 69	SAS

TOTAL SERVICE   15 YEARS 147 DAYS

DECORATIONS, MEDALS AND AWARDS

EFFICIENCY MEDAL (TAVR)

DATE OF DISCHARGE   30 SEP 84

REASON FOR DISCHARGE   PREMATURE DISCHARGE - FREE

OFFICIAL STAMP